Advance Praise for *The SaaS Model*

'In *The SaaS Model*, drawing from his own experience as a senior manager and chief marketing officer, Srinivas offers a detailed step-by-step guide to plan the marketing organisation and process to attain the desired outcomes. A must-read for SaaS practitioners, consultants and senior managers to make SaaS deliver better.'

Joffi Thomas, professor of marketing management, IIM Kozhikode

'*The SaaS Model* by Srinivas is a great read! It analyses SaaS product marketing concepts and compares them with traditional marketing. It will serve as a great piece of reference for SaaS marketers, especially now when SaaS is hot.'

Subhendu Patnaik, principal analyst, Forrester

'As more companies embrace the SaaS model, marketers need to reinvent themselves as full life-cycle marketers, influencing new and expanded motions. This book shows them exactly how.'

Manav Garg, cofounder, SaaSBOOMi, and CEO, Eka Software Solutions

'Srinivas is among the best B2B SaaS marketers in India. I keep turning to him for his advice time and again, and his depth on this subject never fails to impress me. In this book, he brings out amazing insights into the changing landscape of B2B SaaS marketing from his rich experience of building global SaaS businesses. It's a must-read for every SaaS founder and marketer.'

Neeraj Saxena, MD and CEO, Xscale

'Customer experience and success are everyone's responsibility! Marketing engagement and point of view in a SaaS model is becoming very crucial not just in top-of-the-funnel lead generation but also in focused activities during technology adoption which helps with fast-tracking customer maturity and loyalty. I am excited about this book, and it is definitely worth a read when you are considering delighting your customers end to end!'

Revathi Venkatraman, head of APAC Customer Success, Slack

THE SAAS MODEL

A New Dimension to Marketing

Srinivas B. Vijayaraghavan

BLOOMSBURY
NEW DELHI • LONDON • OXFORD • NEW YORK • SYDNEY

BLOOMSBURY INDIA
Bloomsbury Publishing India Pvt. Ltd
Second Floor, LSC Building No. 4, DDA Complex, Pocket C – 6 & 7,
Vasant Kunj, New Delhi 110070

BLOOMSBURY, BLOOMSBURY INDIA and the Diana logo
are trademarks of Bloomsbury Publishing Plc

First published in India 2023
This edition published 2023

ISBN: PB: 978-93-54355-38-7; e-ISBN: 978-93-54355-54-7
2 4 6 8 10 9 7 5 3 1

Typeset in Fournier MT Std by Manipal Technologies Limited
Printed and bound in India

FSC www.fsc.org MIX Paper from responsible sources FSC® C016779

To my parents, Neela and Vijay,
and to my wife, Aishwarya

Contents

Abbreviations

AARRR	Acquisition, Activation, Revenue, Retention, Referral
ABM	Account-based marketing
ACL	Average customer lifetime
ACV	Annual contract value
AI	Artificial intelligence
AIDA	Awareness, interest, decision, action
API	Application programming interface
AR	Analyst relations
ARPA	Average revenue per account
ARR	Annual recurring revenue
AWS	Amazon Web Services
B2B	Business-to-business
BANT	Budget, authority, needs and timeline
BI	Business intelligence
BOFU	Bottom of the funnel
BSP	Business solutions provider
CAC	Customer acquisition cost
CAGR	Compounded annual growth rate
CEO	Chief executive officer
CFO	Chief financial officer
CIO	Chief information officer
CLTV	Customer lifetime value
CM	Community manager
CMO	Chief marketing officer

CPC	Cost per click
CPL	Cost per lead
CPM	Cost per impression
CQL	Conversation qualified lead
CRM	Customer relationship management
CRO	Conversion rate optimisation
CSAT	Customer Satisfaction
CSM	Customer success manager
CTA	Call to action
CTO	Chief technology officer
CX	Customer experience
DevRel	Developer relations
DIFM	Do it for me
DIY	Do it yourself
ERP	Enterprise resource planning
GDP	Gross domestic product
GRR	Gross revenue retention
HCM	Human capital management
HR	Human resources
IDC	International Data Corporation
IIM	Indian Institute of Management
ISV	Independent software vendor
IT	Information technology
KRA	Key responsibility area
MCS	Meaningful connection score
MNC	Multinational company
MOFU	Middle of the funnel
MQL	Marketing qualified lead
MRR	Monthly recurring revenue
MSR	Marketing sourced revenue
NASSCOM	National Association of Software and Service Companies
NPS	Net promoter score

NRR	Net revenue retention
OKR	Objectives and key result
OTT	Over the top
P2P	Person-to-person
PLG	Product-led growth
PM	Project manager
PMM	Product marketing manager
POC	Proof of concept
PQL	Product qualified lead
PR	Public relations
QBR	Quarterly business review
R&D	Research and development
RFI	Request for information
RM	Renewal manager
ROI	Return on investment
S&M	Sales and marketing
SaaS	Software as a service
SCM	Supply chain management
SDR	Sales development representative
SEO	Search engine optimisation
SKU	Stock keeping unit
SMB	Small and midsize business
SMQL	Shadow marketing qualified lead
SMS	Short Message Service
SOI	Sphere of influence
SQL	Sales qualified lead
SSO	Single sign-on
TAM	Total addressable market
TOFU	Top of the funnel
UI	User interface
UMV	Unique monthly visitors
UX	User experience
VP	Vice president

Preface

Between 2020 and 2025, the software as a service (SaaS) market is expected to grow to US$100 billion with a compounded annual growth rate (CAGR) of 11 per cent. SaaS as a business model is a by-product of cloud computing and allows for any service to be provided on the cloud. SaaS provides a subscription-based alternative to the perpetual licence model that has dominated software for the previous two decades. While the industry has grown, several business functions have had to adapt to the 'SaaS way' of doing things, and marketing is one of them. Never has marketing found more relevance in the 'full funnel' of a customer's life cycle from acquisition to renewal than now. SaaS has also led to the rise of new functions such as customer success, which has subsumed and enhanced the customer support model.

India's SaaS market is slated to grow to US$50 billion in revenue by 2025, create a market capitalisation of more than US$1.3 trillion and employ more than 2.6 lakh people, up from 50,000 today. A further 3.5 lakh MBA students pass out of Indian B-schools every year, many of them starting with sales and marketing (S&M) roles. This book aims to provide these professionals and students who are preparing to enter the industry with a guide on how to market a brand in a SaaS world. India has a thriving ecosystem of SaaS enablers, including domestic and global investors, numerous incubators and accelerators (such as xto10x and Upekkha), and events and initiatives sponsored by communities such as the National Association of Software and Service Companies (NASSCOM) and SaaSBOOMi.

This book is designed to be a guide for professional marketers and students preparing for a career in marketing and business development. It provides an overview of how marketing has adapted to the subscription-oriented nature of the SaaS world. We then explore how the classic marketing framework of segmentation, targeting and positioning followed by the 4 Ps is being transformed by data and the availability of a plethora of SaaS-based martech tools. We then map the customer life cycle in SaaS and detail how marketing plays a role in driving the freemium model, how self-service models drive enterprise momentum, how marketing plays a role in enterprise trails and deal acceleration, and how it helps the customer success world with effective onboarding, driving usage and renewing subscriptions.

1

SaaS and Its Impact on Marketing

Understanding the SaaS Business Model

With SaaS, the customer uses the vendor's software over the internet without owning the platform or the underlying infrastructure it runs on. Vendors license their SaaS solutions to customers and provide service and support. In many cases, not all customers get the same level of service and support. Many of them use 'self-service', something that we will touch upon in later chapters. The customer's capital budget is converted into an operating budget. SaaS is relatively lighter on implementation but can get complex based on the number of integrations required.

SaaS allows companies of any size the opportunity to use software because it offers a great deal of strategic and operational flexibility. It also creates a virtuous cycle as it is a business model driven by continuous engagement with the customer. Customers can expect continuous improvements in capabilities and services while they focus on their core business. From a vendor's point of view, a SaaS business model allows for a more predictable revenue stream, regular cash flow and a long-term view of a customer, where product and service roadmaps and innovations can be planned and rolled out more efficiently than in the non-SaaS model.

In their India SaaS 2021 report, Bain Consulting outlined these SaaS themes based on their analysis of both mature and early-stage companies[1]:

1. Horizontal business software: These SaaS companies focus on applications that can be applied across the board—enterprise collaboration, events technology, conversational artificial intelligence (AI) and human resources (HR) technology. The need for data-driven decision-making is driving the growth of business intelligence (BI) and analytics SaaS companies, and AI is proving to be a key component of SaaS feature enhancements.
2. Horizontal infrastructure software: The focus here is on technology systems that can be plugged into a customer's IT infrastructure—cybersecurity, DevOps and development tools, and data management and observability. The rise in cyber attacks and digital transactions is driving the need for data security solutions.
3. Vertical business software: These companies focus on solutions for specific verticals like financial technology (fintech), educational technology (edtech), healthcare technology, logistics technology and e-commerce enablement.
4. Mobile-only SaaS: These companies build native mobile SaaS applications and pursue a mobile-only mindset.

According to NASSCOM, SaaS business models have also evolved due to the proliferation of application programming interfaces (APIs). The API-led SaaS companies offer APIs to help developers build core features for their products like payment processing, customer communication and the like. Unbundled SaaS companies offer SaaS packaged as an API instead of a traditional finished product, enabling users to build their own user experience (UX). Micro-SaaS companies offer products as an extension to existing SaaS products and are run by a single person or a small team within a niche market.

These evolving SaaS business models have had their impact on S&M practices, and they need to evolve from time-tested and cherished methodologies, as we explore in the next section.

Marketing in the Non-SaaS World versus SaaS

Perpetual licences have dominated the software industry for decades. Like hardware, software is sold as a stock keeping unit (SKU). Here, the buyer is provided with a licence to use a version of the software indefinitely after paying an initial lump sum fee. The software licence can come with a support package and a professional services package that can be charged annually and renewed depending on the customer's need.

The role of the marketing function in the non-SaaS world has largely been restricted to driving awareness and enquiries for software products. The heavy lifting, in terms of selling the value of the product, moving the deal through the various stages of the pipeline, closing the deal, onboarding the customer and supporting the customer, has been carried out by sales and support teams. So, marketing has had a top-of-the-funnel (TOFU) responsibility in the non-SaaS world, which has led to a rather disjointed customer experience (CX) where customers are handed over from one function to another as they progress from one stage to the next.

Over the years, marketers have used above-the-line campaigns (TV commercials, radio, outdoor advertising, digital) and below-the-line campaigns (events, outbound phone calls, targeted digital campaigns) to drive awareness and demand for non-SaaS products. The marketing team may reach out to customers later on for surveys and case studies that they use to drive more customers to buy, but that's about it.

Here's how the journey of a customer plays out. A prospective customer attends an event, and their details are recorded and entered into a customer relationship management (CRM) system. The job of the marketing manager is done. The lead is then left to be acted upon by an inside sales team that may or may not be part of the marketing organisation (it usually reports to the sales team). Emails may be sent out with newsletters or offers that may not be customised to the requirements of the prospect. Finally, once the prospect becomes a customer, interaction happens through support helplines and email addresses. The customer-centric view of the process is missing in this approach.

SaaS is different in that a customer can subscribe to a product for a month, a year or even longer but for a predetermined length of time. The product is now a service that the customer can use and stop. The end-to-end customer journey is tracked minutely, and multiple functions, most importantly, the triad of marketing-sales-customer success, play a key role in partnering with customers through their journey. The business motions in SaaS include new, renew and expand. New motions contribute to acquiring a customer for the first time. Renew motions focus on getting the customer to renew their subscription, and expand motions focus on getting the customer to use more advanced and valuable services. SaaS marketing is complete customer life cycle marketing that follows a customer from the prospect stage to the renewal stage and plays a key role in the new, renew and expand motions.

SaaS works like this—further up in the sales cycle, the SaaS marketer partners with the sales team to understand the customers/accounts that they need to acquire, how they can get a 'first touch' through an event or a digital campaign and, more importantly, how they can accelerate the pipeline through the sales process. As the sales team prepares customers for what they are about to subscribe to, the customer success manager (CSM) understands their requirements as they are being sold the product. The marketing manager partners with the sales manager and the CSM to work on onboarding the customer and then getting them to use the service over a twelve-month cycle.

Throughout the twelve-month cycle, the SaaS marketer focuses on upselling new services and capabilities to the customer. In this way, marketing plays a key role in maximising customer lifetime value (CLTV) and optimising the ratio of CLTV to customer acquisition cost (CAC). The SaaS business model is predicated on earning a customer and keeping that customer for a longer period, that is, through multiple renewal and upsell cycles. The CLTV is what the customer spends not just in the first year but over the lifetime of the customer, and the CAC is the average cost incurred to acquire the customer.

Full-Funnel View of Marketing

As the customer moves from being a prospect to signing the deal, SaaS marketing moves from onboarding the customer to getting them to use the service and then renewing the service. This approach is very different from the non-SaaS world where marketing, sales and support are disjointed teams that are loosely coupled, leading to gaps in understanding the customer and information leakages in handing a customer over from one team to another.

A full-funnel view of marketing starts right from the top. There are three parts of the marketing funnel—TOFU, middle of the funnel or MOFU and bottom of the funnel or BOFU. Here, TOFU marketing is about making a prospect aware of your brand. The approach to this phase of the marketing funnel is to get a prospect to learn of the existence of the brand and the services it offers but indirectly. Different tactics are used to attract the prospect to your brand. The first tactic is thought leadership. The prospect is targeted through a series of thought leadership resources related to the work that they do and the best practices to follow.

For example, your SaaS product's target customer may be a marketing manager, and your product helps them to capture leads efficiently on websites. So, thought leadership for this marketing manager would revolve around best practices to reduce friction in the marketing funnel—how do you convert somebody who visits your website to a contact in your CRM system? Now, this thought leadership piece may be a blog post, e-book, podcast episode or YouTube explainer videos. You should not talk about your product or how you can solve the marketing manager's lead generation problem. Instead, you can describe best practices. You can have a form that is easy to fill out. The placement of the form depends on the behaviour of the user. Even though the best practices enabled by your product may be described, the product is not directly mentioned. An indirect association is created in the customer's mind.

Now, this method ties into the traditional marketing concepts of brand recognition and brand recall. Brand recognition is about recognising a brand name. Whether or not you recognise a brand is a binary question and can be answered with a yes or no. Brand recall is whether you think of a brand when you think of a particular problem that you face or when you're in a purchasing scenario. In SaaS, TOFU activities try to solve both awareness and recall problems but in a non-sales manner. The focus is on building trust with the prospect by 'giving' before 'asking'.

Another way to build thought leadership is to invite people to listen in or participate in conversations about challenges in their line of work or industry. Invite your prospects to events where they can either participate as speakers or learn from the speakers of the panel that you have assembled. Again, you should not present your product capability or try to sell anything. The attempt is to make your prospect aware of your brand and then help them associate their awareness with a recall. Whenever they think of a problem in the space in which you operate, they should think of your brand. So, apart from content, leveraging events is another interesting way of connecting with prospects as a SaaS marketer.

Now you may think that these are standard tactics that are prevalent in the non-SaaS world or even in the traditional marketing world, but what happens after that is where the full-funnel view of marketing kicks in. We looked at the three stages of marketing. Usually, TOFU tactics do not give actionable leads. So people may be interested in your content, download a white paper, subscribe to your podcast or a feed of a digest of your blog posts, but they are not ready to buy from you. As a SaaS marketer, you should not assume that they are.

Next, there is a departure from the non-SaaS world. In the non-SaaS world, after generating leads, you hand them over to a team that calls the customers or sends them an email blast or does five programmed follow-up calls in the next two or three weeks to see if they're interested in buying a solution. These methods of dealing with a prospect to gauge whether they're interested or not are binary.

In SaaS, a prospect is taken on a journey and put through a nurture programme. A nurture programme is typically run through an email sequence or by retargeting on social media. You should make sure that this particular person continues to receive something of value from your brand that they continue to find useful. Somewhere in their subconscious, they create a space for you. While you can't measure a person's mind, what they think of you manifests in the way they react to the stimuli that you send them. If you assign a value to each of their interactions and add them up over a period, you will know whether they are warming up to you or not. This method is called lead scoring.

Lead scoring tracks how interested customers are in interacting with you across stimuli that you subject them to. The stimulus could be a newsletter with a subscribe button or an email about a solution that you sent them or a webinar invitation. Whether they open your email, sign up for a webinar, click on something that you sent or return to your website to browse some more, each of these activities is given a score, and as the score points accumulate, your lead qualifies to move from TOFU to MOFU. The prospect now moves from being aware to developing an interest in what your solution can do for them. As you can imagine, TOFU deserves all the time and planning to ensure that the maximum number of your buyer personas become aware of your brand and enter the wheelhouse.

The MOFU tactics focus on converting an aware customer into an interested customer, similar to the awareness-interest-decision-action process. The prospect's decision is not reduced to a binary yes or no. If the person is allowed to figure out more about you, when they get to a point where they are ready to explore or buy, they will come back to you. The SaaS marketer now focuses on sharing anecdotes and stories, including case studies, testimonials and explainer videos on products, on how the subscription helped someone similar to the prospect solve a problem. The prospect is also invited to product webinars. Depending on their response, they may be given a chance to try the subscription for free, so that they can explore it for themselves. If they respond, then they enter the BOFU.

BOFU is when the prospect is sufficiently interested through the top and middle order for the SaaS marketer to give them the final set of nudges to get them talking budget, authority, needs and timeline (BANT) with either a sales development representative (SDR) or with inside sales. At this point, the lead becomes a marketing qualified lead (MQL), and once the SDR qualifies it further with BANT, it becomes a sales qualified lead (SQL) and moves to the top of the sales pipeline.

The key point to note in the prospect's journey is that the marketer has to design the nurture programme in such a way that the prospect continues to get richer and deeper information about the company as he or she moves through the funnel. In a way, you write a script and orchestrate the prospect through a journey where you start with simple, generic and useful insights about a problem that a prospect might face, and then move into more interesting solutions that your brand offers. Finally, you get them to a point where they are ready to commit to you.

Speaking of lead scoring, marketing automation went from just automating emails to automating the whole lead orchestration process. Today, millions of prospects are being nurtured across the world through completely personalised journeys. This holistic lead orchestration process is one of the biggest contributions of SaaS to the way marketers look at the buyer's life cycle.

During the qualification process, different companies use different formats. One such format is BANT qualification, where you check for budget, authority, need and timeline. This process can be done manually or it can be automated in the lead generation process where the prospect is asked a set of questions and is then passed on to the SDR to accelerate qualification. However, another common method in the SaaS model is to get the prospect to try your platform for free. Some call it a pilot, test drive or freemium. The prospect signs up for an experience that gives them a sense of what your platform and your solution feel like. This experience could be in a preconfigured environment depending on the kind of solution that you have that they can plug into and use. They may even take their own data or information and plug it into a business preconfigured environment to see what it looks like.

In the SaaS model, there is a divergence at this point, called self-service (also called self-serv). The prospect tries out your solution, uses it on their own and pays for it on your website or mobile app. Once they sign up, they go into a guided motion where the platform guides them on which features to use and suggests upgrades for more premium features. SaaS marketers have a key role to play in co-designing the sales experience with the product team.

In the more traditional sales process, prospects go through the qualification stage and the sales pipeline, but the SaaS marketer's job is not done. The prospect has to be continuously engaged throughout the sales process as well. Here, the primary focus of engagement is sales acceleration towards closure. The SaaS marketer needs to continue to nurture the prospect, invite them to important conferences and webinars that the company organises and get them into panel discussions or roundtables in which current customers already participate. While they evaluate the software, the nurturing instils confidence that they are working with the right kind of company.

The SaaS marketer is part of a quad consisting of the sales, business development, marketing and customer success teams. When a customer chooses to go to the managed model, the sales, customer success and pre-sales teams get involved in building the solution and closing the deal with the customer. The SaaS marketer has to partner with the customer success team as the customer comes on board.

So every step of the process has to be a partnership between the customer success team and the marketing team. If users get an effective onboarding, they get to use the product and understand how to make the best use of it. Onboarding is crucial because depending on the kind of business you are in, not all users actually log in and start to use the service. There could be multiple reasons—they have many choices of other services or the legacy that they use or they may not be incentivised to use your platform now. In cases where an employer subscribes to your platform for hundreds or thousands of their employees, getting everyone to onboard and use the platform is even more challenging.

SaaS businesses are built on renewals. So the CLTV depends on how many renewal cycles take place, which depends on how the service is consumed. So, as a SaaS marketer, your shared responsibility is to ensure that users are excited about using the service and that they know what it's all about. Hence, partnering with customer success during the initial onboarding phase as soon as the customer comes on board is necessary.

The process doesn't stop there, because usage monitoring is essential during a twelve-month cycle of a subscription service. Usage monitoring is a key customer success parameter, but the customer success team also needs help from the marketing team to ensure that users are shown how they can use the different features of the service, both basic and advanced, and how, if they start with one part of your feature set, they get to explore another part of your feature set.

Sometimes, the challenge is to get customers to use the service more and more if it is a consumption-based service. Here, the marketing team needs to work on usage-based campaigns, gamify usage, run hackathons and create internal company-wide events to get people excited about using the platform. These activities help customer success and drive a good usage rate throughout the twelve-month cycle. At some point in the twelve-month cycle, usually the third or fourth quarter, your sales teams start looking at renewal. Renewal is an activity that involves both inputs from the users, who must say that they like the service and want to use it, and decision makers, who take a call on the renewal, possibly the same people who signed up the first time.

Additionally, the procurement and finance teams could get involved at this point, but the key decision is always with the business users of the subscription. Here, the SaaS marketing team partners with the sales team. Whether you work with the hunting or farming sales teams, you need to follow the same process of warming up your alpha users and making them influencers for your service. The decision makers should also be warmed up to say that they want to renew the subscription and are open to discussions on continuing the service for another twelve-month cycle or possibly a twenty-four-month cycle.

The other motion that works very well in SaaS is called an expand motion. With expand, you try to upgrade the customer from one level of service to another level of service. You started with a basic set of features, and now you want them to try out the advanced features. Exciting the customers about what they can explore with the platform works very well. SaaS marketers can also show and tell to demonstrate how other customers have tried the subscription and solved their business challenges. Nothing works for a customer better than them knowing that somebody in their peer group or the competitive set has adopted something and that it has helped them. Thus, a SaaS marketer can impact the expand motion.

The Triad and the Quad

SaaS marketers never work in isolation. We saw how the marketing function assumes a full customer life cycle role. In this scenario, marketing has to partner with other functions that play a role in a customer's life cycle—sales, customer success, solutions architecture/pre-sales and inside sales. For business-to-business (B2B) SaaS companies, account-based marketing (ABM) becomes crucial. This sales model has lent itself to the world of marketing. The ABM approach has a razor-sharp marketing focus on acquiring a set of named targeted accounts chosen by the sales team, which are the most important accounts to either acquire, expand or renew for the growth of the business. In the SaaS world, ABM requires the sales, marketing, customer success and solutions architecture teams to work in a set of three (triad) or four (quad).

A triad is the simplest collaboration unit and involves a marketer, an account manager and a CSM. Account managers bring in the sales perspective and identify the key accounts that they need to acquire, expand or renew. The CSMs are responsible for helping customers use and derive success from the product. The CSMs help to craft strategies for expansion and renewal and also work to be ready when a particular account is going through its final stages of negotiation before they come on board. The quad is an extension of the triad and includes a solutions architect or pre-sales. The quad becomes essential when the product or service that a brand sells in a SaaS model is complex and requires technical competency to help the prospect appreciate the features and benefits.

Forming triads and quads requires greater organisational collaboration across multiple functions. Therefore, at a leadership level, the sales, customer success, marketing and product teams need to work hand-in-hand and transparently. The process of forming triads and quads should start ideally around the time of annual planning, which is usually at any point in the last 25 per cent of a calendar year. During the annual planning process, the sales organisation identifies the accounts and the segments that they would like to target, driven by the company's strategy and growth goals. The customer success organisation creates a plan to grow revenues from existing customers as compared to the previous year and the kind of initiatives that need to be driven within existing accounts. The technology teams identify the key products and features that are going to be launched in the subsequent year at various stages of the product life cycle. Finally, the marketing team absorbs all these inputs and adds to it the broad themes that the SaaS brand takes to market in the coming calendar year.

Once there is alignment at the leadership level, the triad and quad structure needs to percolate down to middle management and individual contributors. So, ideally, a triad or a quad should be assigned to every sales territory in the organisation irrespective of where they are in the world. The structuring of the organisation has to be more open, with tight interlocks between different functions at the senior, middle and junior levels.

Once the organisational structure and the triad and quad structures are in place, there has to be a continual interlock between members of the groups on a daily and weekly basis. Account reviews are no longer to be done just to the sales team but need to involve representatives of three or four teams together. Account strategies are jointly conceived, executed and tracked.

Triads and Quads for New Customer Acquisition

Thinking about triads and quads may be counterintuitive when the customer is not yet a part of the system. However, if you take a full life cycle view of a customer, targeting the prospect organisation even before they become customers is important. In this phase of the customer life cycle, the marketer takes the lead. The marketer understands the account, the decision makers, the chief economic buyers, the influencers and other members of the buying centre and proceeds to craft an acquisition plan that uses a combination of field and digital marketing tactics from the SaaS marketing tool box.

As the prospect progresses through the top, the middle and the bottom of the marketing funnel, the marketer starts working with the CSM and the account manager to initiate the prospect into an expected experience mode. The prospect may be invited to a workshop where the CSM conducts a mock exercise on mapping the product features to the prospect's requirements. The prospect may also be invited to speak at certain exclusive events that the marketer has organised where the CSM and account manager are also present physically or virtually.

As the prospect navigates through the sales funnel from the marketing funnel, the role of the account manager becomes more prominent, followed by the CSM, and the marketer takes a backseat but plays more of a supporting role. In this phase, the focus is on how the economic buyer is kept motivated while going through the process of evaluation. Relevant information must be shared with the economic buyer about other customers who have experienced success, success metrics that other customers have seen and quotes and testimonials that other customers have provided. Also, broad metrics on how different segments of customers have fared after investing in this product or service must be showcased. The CSM also starts preparing for the onboarding part of the journey as the probability of the deal closure increases as the prospect moves towards the sales cycle.

Triads and Quads for Expansion

Triads and quads are key drivers of the expansion business. Expansion is the core of the SaaS business model and completely drives and sustains business growth. Once the customer is onboarded and goes through, for example, the first year of the subscription, the CSM takes over and looks at usage and, more importantly, upselling and cross-selling more services or the same services to more users within the customer account. Given that an account manager has multiple accounts to acquire and cater to, the

CSM becomes the de facto voice of the customer within the client's organisation.

The CSMs have an intimate knowledge of the economic buyers, the power users and the influencers and also become aware of latent demand within the customer account. Armed with this information and insight, they partner with the account manager and the marketer to look at the account as a segment in itself, a segment of one. The marketer segments the buying centre within the account and proceeds to work on a set of marketing campaigns that serve one of several objectives:

1. Building or strengthening relationships with current economic buyers
2. Ensuring that a larger set of customer employees know about the brand and the service being provided
3. Ensuring that users are happy and are rewarded for their usage through usage-driving campaigns
4. Expanding the sphere of influence (SOI) of the SaaS brand within the customer account

The expansion motion typically kicks in after the first quarter or the second quarter of usage. Usually, SaaS companies aim for their sales organisations to achieve anywhere between 40 and 60 per cent of the base contract value in expansion. To achieve this level of growth, the triad and the quad must work together to ensure that the SOI is expanded within the account, more economic buyers are brought into the sales pipeline and enough credibility and strength are built in the relationship to ensure that expansion takes place. The advantage of the expansion motion is that it can take place at any point in the subscription year, even mid-year or mid-cycle. This reduces the pressure of renewals combined with expansion, something we will address in the next section.

Triads and Quads for Renewals

Renewal is the greatest sustainer of a SaaS business. While expansion powers growth, renewal keeps the business going. The triad and the quad need to start working at least three to six months before the date of renewal to ensure a successful outcome. In the SaaS world, renewal rates of 95 to 97 per cent are not uncommon. Two terms that drive renewals are gross revenue retention (GRR) and net revenue retention (NRR). The GRR asks how many customers and how much revenue has been retained. The GRR looks at the ability of a SaaS business to retain customers, while NRR is the percentage of revenue retained from existing customers including renewals and expansions. SaaS companies aim for an NRR greater than 100 per cent and GRR closer to 100 per cent.

One of the key drivers of a successful renewal is customer satisfaction (CSAT). While the CSM keeps a finger on the pulse of every customer account, the SaaS marketer has a key role to play to ensure that the users of the service are motivated to use it and achieve their business objectives while using it. Renewal begins with onboarding. If the onboarding experience is not efficient, the probability of a successful renewal starts lowering. The SaaS marketer partners with the CSM to create an efficient onboarding process involving account-based events, training sessions, gamification for driving usage and a variety of other tactics. The first quarter of engagement activities is crucial for renewal three quarters later.

As the first net promoter score (NPS) and the CSAT score come in, the SaaS marketer needs to focus on low users and non-users. This segment of users has either not activated the service or has not used it at all. The marketer needs to devise effective tactics to ensure that those who have not used the service use it and those who are using it well become champions of it within the organisation and outside the organisation.

The key players in a renewal decision must be noted. The economic buyers who sign off on the service in a new motion need not be the same set that signs off during the renewal motion. While the finance and procurement teams play a role in both new motions and renewal motions, the influencers in the new motion were the set of power users or evaluators, but the influencers in the renewed motion are satisfied users and they may be numerous. The CSMs find it hard to have an SOI or a direct connection with hundreds and, sometimes, even thousands of users with an account. However, in partnership with the marketing team, they keep a finger on the pulse of usage at all times.

A few months before the renewal, the key players in the renewal decision-making are identified, and the marketer participates in quarterly business reviews (QBRs) and showcases the impact of the service to the customer account. Marketers can also make champions of the buyers and influencers in a third-party forum where buyers or users are projected as innovators because they have used the service for the betterment of their organisation.

Triads and Quads in Self-Service Motions

By definition, self-service does not require a triad or quad motion. However, the way the CX in a self-service motion is designed can lend itself to timely intervention by members of the triad or quad. The experience should be instrumented to understand how users go about using the service on their own.

Triggers can be enabled to get either a customer support intervention or, if the usage is high, a sales intervention or, if there is a customised requirement, a customer service or customer success intervention. Marketing has a role to play by designing the experience with the right set of nudges to help the user explore the platform, use it more and also nurture the user in an automated fashion to try and move into an enterprise sales motion. A close partnership between the product engineering CX team and the marketing team is required. The marketer can also create in-product nudges and advertisements for upselling and cross-selling across the feature set.

2

Customer Acquisition and the Freemium Model

Product-Led Growth

From a marketing point of view, understanding product-led growth (PLG) is important. PLG makes the product the primary driver of customer acquisition, conversion and expansion. According to Variance's Global PLG Index, Stripe, Canva, Plaid, Figma and Zapier are the top five PLG companies in the world and grow faster and more efficiently by leveraging their products by creating a pipeline of active users who then graduate to becoming paying customers. The PLG approach can be adopted by any kind of company but requires transparent pricing and a freemium model to be in place. A large driver of the PLG era has been the shift in buying power from 'economic buyer' to 'end user'. The democratisation of software has made it more accessible to users, who now expect to use it, play with it and build on top of it with more ease than ever before. The role of marketing has evolved as the buying power for technology products and solutions has shifted through different balances of power.

Technology Leader Is the Buyer

Hardware and associated software were sold, bought, installed and run as physical installations on the customer's premises. The decision makers were usually the heads of the information technology (IT) functions, the chief information officers (CIOs). Most software and hardware vendors have pursued the CIO organisation and chief technology officer (CTO) organisation over the last thirty years in a 'sales-led growth' motion. The marketing team's role here is to partner with the sales team to connect with and influence the technology buyer organisation. As we will explore later, this model persists in the SaaS era.

Business/Functional Leader Is the Buyer

With the emergence of the cloud, technology emerged from the IT world into the functional world, where buyer personas like marketers, product managers (PMs), finance heads and supply chain heads became users of technology. For sales teams and marketing teams, this development meant targeting the non-technical executive, and the focus was more on results, returns and measurements, rather than just features. SaaS also emerged during this phase as did 'marketing-led growth', where marketers generated MQLs and SDRs qualified them and powered sales teams forward.

The End User Is the Buyer/Key Influencer

As the cloud proliferated, so did 'open architectures' that encouraged companies to expose APIs to their platforms so that other companies could integrate with them. Most SaaS companies have open architectures because their product has to integrate with the existing technology and business technology stack of the customer. Developers and end users were brought to the fore as they worked together to define and implement the technology capability that they need. For these personas, the decision to buy is not based on how the product features provide a return on investment (ROI) but on how the product helps them in *their* everyday tasks and requirements. The marketing challenge in this scenario is to engage with a broadly dispersed set of individuals instead of a concentrated set of end users. This challenge has influenced marketers to create scalable marketing programmes that target end users and developers and a product design that enables individuals to try, experiment, play with and then decide.

OpenView's Blake Bartlett first defined 'product-led growth' in 2016:

> There is an inexorable march toward the End User Era that simply can't be stopped. As a software company, you can't opt out of this secular shift. It's pretty damn obvious that you wouldn't build an on-prem product geared for the CIO Era. While you can still get away with building your business for the Exec Era, that wave has already crested and its days are numbered. The End User Era is here. Product-led growth is how you thrive in it.[2]

How Can SaaS Marketers Adapt to a PLG Environment?

1. Influence design for end users: Work with product teams to interview end users, and conduct user interface (UI) walkthroughs and experiments to provide an outside-in perspective to product management and design teams.
2. Help deliver a great trial experience: PLG companies allow users to access some or all of the product before they need to pay, often through a self-serve free trial, freemium model or open-source model. Marketing can help design a great product experience that leads to an aha moment for the user.

3. Build go-to-market dimensions within the product: Marketing can help equip the product with robust product data that allows teams to track, measure and analyse user behaviour and can run go-to-market experiments that lead to incremental improvements to the user journey. Metrics that marketers measure in PLG companies include growth rates, payback on CACs, the ratio of CLTV to CACs and logo retention. We will explore all of these in subsequent chapters.

Try to Get the Freemium Model

The freemium model is one of the most important growth engines of a SaaS business. In a non-SaaS business, we call this model a try and buy, something that's quite prevalent in the consumer world as well. The freemium model is predicated on the belief that a customer would want to use the service before they take a call on subscribing to it. It is a frictionless process in which a prospect can be allowed into the very early stages of the sales pipeline with almost no intervention from anybody in the sales process. Freemium models come in a variety of shapes and sizes.

A true freemium model would allow a user to use a service for a limited period with no commitment to adding a credit card or being charged at the end of it. This version is the most basic and is found on most SaaS websites. The usage is typically limited to a few iterations or transactions, and there is a paywall. The model usually involves a limited version of the product that makes it partially usable. Overuse of this model expends a lot of resources because of the cost to serve, and hence, a view on ROI must always be maintained. This freemium model tends to have extreme difficulty converting customers from a free version to paid version. This challenge can also be called the 'penny gap'.

A freemium model with a guarantee of payment at the end of the free period would have the user share financial information at the start of the period and then be charged once that period ends, but they would have the option to cancel at any time during the free period. This method encourages users to think before they act and might provide a better balance between cost to serve and ROI extraction from a freemium model.

A pilot programme is a freemium model applied to larger deals in the enterprise world where you have a set of power users using the service for a fixed time. This model has an evaluation period at the end of the free period where the users evaluate the service. The SaaS company and the customer get an opportunity to sit down and discuss the merits and demerits of going ahead. Pilots can be paid as well if the vendor and customer agree to this beforehand.

The freemium model also extends into a 'land and expand' strategy, which involves getting individual users within an organisation to sign up for a product for free and monetising the product at the organisational level. Companies like Trello by Atlassian use this model well. Slack and Yammer also get users within a company to sign up for free and, once a certain threshold is hit, convert the organisation into a paid subscription.

Forever-free fully functional models allow users to use the full-feature product for free and charge for additional features or power users. WeTransfer is a good example of this model as is Skype. Mobile games also use this model and charge users to speed up games or for game extensions.

Freemium models can also be used when an established brand wants to introduce a new feature or product line. Companies get a foot in the door without having to do a direct upsell. CRM companies use this strategy when they add marketing capabilities or customer success capabilities to their suite. Marketing automation companies also use it when they expand into having a CRM of their own.

Ecosystem models also use a free base product and monetise it through integrations with third-party developers. An app store or Google Play Store would use this. Some companies use the network effect by offering the full product to millions of users and leverage traffic, data and insights to serve companies through advertising platforms. Meta, Google and the like use this model.

Companies also build free tools that users find helpful and, once they use them enough, offer paid versions of their software. CoSchedule's headline analyser tool is a good example. There are several website analysis tools as well. Companies use these tools like marketing 'assets'.

The freemium model provides SaaS businesses with multiple benefits:

1. Provides value and then derives value
2. Acquires contact information in a frictionless manner when customers sign in and can capture additional information as they continue to use
3. Lowers CAC
4. Tests your product and new features before you make it available to everyone
5. Builds an NPS from users, which can encourage others to explore

There is a flip side, of course:

1. Moving free users to paid users may prove difficult, depending on the freemium model you choose.

2. The cost to serve free users can balloon, especially if you are using third-party cloud hosting services like Amazon Web Services (AWS) or Google Cloud or Azure.

User First, Customer Next

SaaS business growth is built on usage. In the non-SaaS world, whether licences were used or not did not matter. Creating a need for the product and keeping the renewals coming in were crucial. However, the freemium model as explained in the previous section helps SaaS businesses court users to try the product before they can buy or convince the economic buyers to buy. The design of a freemium model needs to be about 'self service' as much as possible because of the costs and dependency on resources to support multiple non-paying users.

However, self-service need not apply to all features of your product or all customer segments. Therefore, segmenting your customers is critical for identifying how best to incorporate self-service. Key questions to ask include which features provide value to new users, which ones require the least amount of support and which customer segments can be tapped into while using the free service. To build an effective self-service experience, the following steps can be followed.

Understanding the End User

What does success look like for the end user while using your product? Who is the persona (an accountant or a marketer or a procurement manager)? What is the goal they want to achieve while using your product (start a campaign, complete a design or convert a document)? Is there a moment in the experience where they feel that they have received value (a campaign launched, an order placed or a payment made)? Is there a usage level that qualifies them to be converted to paid users?

Create the Customer Journey and Measure with the Right Success Metrics

Given that self-service by definition runs programmatically, instrumenting the experience with the right metrics that tell you how much a user uses the freemium features, how effectively they use it and also how easy or hard they find the UX is essential. Defining the key life cycle events in the user journey is also important. If your product helps a campaign manager set up a messaging campaign on WhatsApp, the life cycle could be to create a WhatsApp business account, upload the target list, add a message, test the message and send a campaign.

Nudge Users towards Key Events

Once the events are clear, users should be nudged to go through them. The key is to remove friction and distractions and design the UI to make the steps crystal clear to a user. In case they need help, provide them with videos, demonstrations and content that they can use to resolve their queries. In case users step out of the product experience without going through the key moments, leverage email automation to use behaviour-based nudges. Using the same example as the WhatsApp campaign, if a user has just logged in but not created anything and logged out, an email can be sent that says, 'You haven't created your first campaign yet. Log in to try'. Using marketing automation systems such as Marketo and HubSpot, to name a few, user interactions with each such email can be tracked and used to build the user profile.

For active users, emails should help them use all the freemium features and also ask for feedback or reviews. This automation reduces the pressure on support teams.

Focus on Good Design to Minimise Support Requirements

Good design can go a long way in helping SaaS companies minimise support resource commitments, especially for freemium users. Here are a few things to remember.

Make Your Product Easily Discoverable

Users need to be able to find the product almost immediately upon visiting your website. Self-service needs to be integrated into the information architecture of the website and must feel like an extension of the pre-login experience. Making information easily searchable within your website is equally important.

Make the UI Simple

The UX does not need glamour and clutter but a meaningful UI that is simple to understand and use by someone skilled/unskilled in the art. Choices should be minimised. Instead of catering to all possibilities, only what the user will probably use should be offered, removing anything that does not add value to the journey of events that you want the user to take. Features that can be found when needed can be hidden. SaaS marketers can play a huge role in providing an outside-in perspective to product design.

Provide Help

Help should be provided in the form of content. Keep frequently asked questions, demonstrations and videos handy, as well as access to a community of users who are keen on helping others learn the product. In case all else fails and the user needs to find help, automated tools like chatbots can be used, and finally, live agent support should be provided to cover less than 5 per cent of all user queries. Content should be easy to read and written plainly, without jargon and to the point. Users need to find the information quickly or else it leads to frustration.

Personalising the Experience

Building a connection with a user can be improved by personalising the UX in a way that goes beyond just using the user's first name to welcome them. Apart from that, using a customer data platform to track how the user has been using the product will also help personalise the UX. Personalised experiences build loyalty and create familiarity for the user with the SaaS platform. Platforms usually do not force users to re-enter login information when they are already logged in or they use single sign-on (SSO) as a login experience.

Improving the Experience

Getting feedback from users is critical to improving the effectiveness of the product. This process also eliminates creator biases, which can creep in if you've spent months and years building the product. The following list provides a high-level overview of tools and approaches:

1. User satisfaction surveys can be provided as in-product experiences
2. NPS allows users to tell you how likely they are to promote you to their network
3. Product analytics provide compelling insights that can drive better design

4. Gathering customer feedback on individual answers lets certain satisfied/dissatisfied users be hand-picked to provide feedback

The other way to improve UX is to measure the abandonment of the objective by the user. The success of the self-service experience is measured by the ratio of the number of users who complete the journey to those who start it. It can also be measured by how many times users checked for content and used the answers to achieve success as defined by the customer journey.

Altering Mental Models of Usage

If picking up the phone and talking to a live agent is something that users are attuned to doing, that habit is hard to change but can be done with the intelligent use of behavioural nudges and information architecture. If you want users to find their own answers, then phone numbers should not be easily available and searchable. Erecting these types of barriers alone is not enough because they can cause user frustration. Users need to be trained to not think of speaking to a live agent as the preferred mode but to figure things out for themselves. One way to do it is to reward them with compliments like 'Yay! You have created your account, let's move forward'. The other way is to give them badges for crossing different milestones—'You have just won the explorer badge for having set up your first campaign'. These methods create a reward mechanism around being able to help oneself.

Proof of Concepts and Pilots

Not all SaaS products are easy to use and configure. Some of them require a different type of try-and-buy model, where a set of prospective users try out the product and test a variety of factors before making a purchase decision. Enter proof of concept (POC), which lies between trials and pilots. So, POCs are more formal and goal-oriented than pilots and have active participation from the SaaS vendor. The objective of a POC is to show how the solution works for a specific use case and that the promised benefits are realised. It also serves as a baseline for wider usage within the client organisation. They are usually paid projects and are set for neither too short nor too long a duration to avoid them becoming full-fledged projects.

The POCs are useful exercises to evaluate new features and technologies that a client might not be familiar with. The results of POCs can be used to get more stakeholders in the buying centre aligned and to rationalise the decision that a couple of stakeholders may already have made in their minds. When POCs are done right, they provide immeasurable confidence to decision makers and influencers. However, POCs focus mainly on proving functionality and testing integrations, not necessarily on scale and performance.

Pilots, on the other hand, are what lie between POCs and a production roll-out. In a pilot phase, the SaaS solution is rolled out to a subset of the final number of users, say 10 per cent, and is evaluated on an almost live scale to see if there are issues and concerns with the pilot group. Pilots provide the following advantages:

1. Validation of the solution in an almost-live environment
2. Implementation gap identification and revelation of real areas where improvement is needed
3. Creation of buy-ins across the client organisation with successful pilots, which drives stakeholder support across the entire organisation

Shadow Funnel and Shadowing the Pipeline

While it is customary to think of terms like funnel and pipeline when it comes to demand generation for a SaaS business, these concepts do not capture the concept of 'intent' when it is shown outside the purview of the brand. In a SaaS business, the sales pipeline is fed, to a large extent, by the marketing funnel and the rest by outbound prospecting by sales and inside sales teams. A marketing funnel mirrors the classic buying stages—awareness, interest, decision, action (AIDA)—and takes a prospect through this journey until they are ready to talk to a sales/ inside sales representative in your company.

1. Awareness: Do they know you and the solution you provide?
2. Consideration: Are they evaluating your solution for their need?
3. Decision: Are they taking a decision on using your solution for their need?

However, all of these factors capture intent as it is demonstrated within your system, be it a website, mobile app, chatbot, landing page, webinar, tradeshow or office. However, they do not capture the intent that is displayed *even before* they interact with you and *even after* they interact with you after leaving your properties and going to other places to learn more. A shadow funnel is said to exist then.

A shadow MQL (SMQL) is one where a prospect shows interest and initiative in your product category and possibly with one or more of your competitors but not you. Tools like ZoomInfo, 6sense, Demandbase and G2 (formerly G2 Crowd), to name a few, can give you credible insight into which companies intend to look for solutions that you offer. Once the intent is established, identifying the next best action is important. Most of the intent information is at a company level. So a mapping needs to be done between your persona database and the companies with intent, or audiences need to be built on digital channels where persona and account combined can be targeted. Intent data is also integrated with standard pipeline stages as a part of 'data enrichment'. Intent data indicates that an account in the pipeline stage 'proposal' stage, say, is scoring high on purchasing intent. This knowledge can be used to forecast deals and revenue for the company more accurately.

In managing a funnel, prospects are moved down the funnel and various activities are designed to nudge and nurture them towards BOFU where they take a call on purchase. Awareness campaigns drive TOFU contact capture, while nurture campaigns and retargeting campaigns focus on pipeline acceleration and movement to the funnel bottom. When it comes to the shadow funnel, the goal is to move them from the shadow to the real funnel or to move them out of the shadows and into the light. One way to think of a shadow funnel is to look at all the companies that form part of your total addressable market (TAM) that are not part of your marketing or sales funnel. The focus is to move those who have a shadow awareness towards your brand and for those who are in a shadow decision phase to consider your SaaS brand for their needs.

Every funnel has a top, a middle and a bottom part. Each part is narrower than the previous part, and each part represents growing intent towards consideration and decision. The marketing funnel is similarly composed of TOFU, MOFU and BOFU. SaaS marketers need to have a full-funnel view that traverses the S&M pipeline, which brings us to the topic of pipeline acceleration.

A key aspect of having a life cycle view of a customer is to be a co-traveller with the customer through the pipeline. Many companies think that the marketing team's role stops at lead generation and lead qualification. They miss out on the important aspect of pipeline acceleration. Pipeline acceleration is an ABM strategy to accelerate the pace of an account moving through the sales funnel. The goal of pipeline acceleration is to increase efficiency in managing the pipeline and realising revenue. Pipeline acceleration needs a close partnership with S&M teams so that key stakeholders are identified and key milestones in the sales process are identified and mapped to events like trails, POCs and pilots. Pipeline acceleration can be measured by time to revenue as a metric and by the decrease in the time taken by a prospect to become a paying customer.

To achieve pipeline acceleration, SaaS marketers need to work with the sales team to create acceleration campaigns. For instance, mapping key decision makers is done early in the pipeline, and the marketing team focuses on nurturing them with BOFU content and inviting them to participate as speakers in webinars and round tables. Typically, decision makers visit vendor websites to seek more information. Tracking their presence on websites and creating richer profiles of activity on the CRM is a key step. Tools like Demandbase and 6sense help you do this. Based on this, multichannel touches and personalisation can be created when it comes to website experience or email nurtures. As the prospect moves closer to a decision, the marketing activity needs to increase but in a subtle, non-intrusive manner. This way, the marketing team partners with the sales team and also the customer, deep into the sales pipeline.

However, pipeline acceleration also starts from the very top of the funnel. The marketing team can help to fill the top of the pipeline with targeted, qualified leads that have a greater propensity to move rapidly through the funnel. The targeting mechanism, lead nurture mechanism and content marketing mechanism must be on point for the persona that is being nurtured. Offers that help to move dormant prospects or nudge late-stage prospects to close are also quite useful in accelerating the pipeline and helping increase sales velocity. For this, the S&M teams need to sign off on account lists. Using the martech stack, marketers can determine if any of these accounts are already part of the shadow funnel like we saw in the previous section, and those accounts can be targeted with more marketing resources. Predictive analytics provides probabilities on the propensity to buy by scoring accounts that are in the pipeline based on their shadow funnel activity. Such analytics provide more insight to the sales team, and they can give more attention to such accounts.

Marketing attribution models cause varying levels of discomfort to those that consume it. The discomfort arises due to the plausibility of the influence having taken place.

Here are a few:

1. First touch: A million-dollar deal is attributed to a white paper downloaded three years prior. There is major disbelief as all intermediate steps are ignored.
2. Last touch: A million-dollar deal is attributed to the last interaction the prospect had—an email open on a case study nurture. This is more believable than the first touch and is better for web conversions but doesn't give credit for earlier lead nurturing.
3. Linear attribution: All interactions are equal with equal weights assigned to all. This idea is far-fetched as a

CX event and a white paper download are not created equal. A variant is the time decay model where touches closer to the closure are given more weights.

4. U-shaped, W-shaped and Z-shaped attributions: More weightage is given to first contact, lead creation, opportunity creation and opportunity closure, and the rest is distributed among other touches. This attribution is widely used as the most plausible method.

There's no perfect model. The most important approach is to get a buy-in from the sales team and executive leadership on the model used and ideally build one that suits the dynamics of your business.

3

Nurturing and the Role of Content

Acquire Once, Nurture over Time

Technology in marketing has enabled the concept of retargeting and nurturing. What this means is that your engagement with prospects or a customer is not limited to the first instance only. The first instance of them clicking your ad, visiting your website or filling out a form and downloading an asset is merely the beginning of a long journey where the SaaS marketer nurtures the prospect and gives them stimuli to get them to warm up to the brand. This process is consistent with the AIDA framework where you move a prospect from awareness to interest to decision and action, but nurturing brings the whole process to life.

Without nurturing, the first touch that a prospect has with the brand becomes the most important step that he or she takes in the interaction with that brand. The interaction could be attending an event or downloading an asset or visiting a website. The onus was placed on that first touch. That first touch had to make sure that the prospect was sufficiently hooked for him or her to be engaged by an inside sales or sales team. However, in reality, prospects don't become customers overnight. Especially with the advent of the internet and comparison sites and a ton of information available online, prospects like to take the time to decide on whether to engage with a brand or not. We discussed this in the shadow funnel section. Prospects tend to research a lot outside the funnel without the marketer even knowing it. So retargeting and nurturing play a key role in keeping an equation going with the prospect.

Let us look at what retargeting means. Retargeting, also known as remarketing, is a marketing activity specifically focused on an audience that you know has visited your website before. Today, the activity is most commonly associated with online display advertisements. After a visitor views your website, they will see your display advertisement appear on other sites across the internet. However, retargeting can also be extended to other channels such as email.

Retargeting refers to the act of serving advertisements based on a searcher's previous browsing history. How does this happen? A 'cookie' or 'pixel' is a snippet of code that allows an advertisement network to display advertisements to anyone who has visited a website, opened an email or been exposed to other assets where these code snippets can be inserted into a landing page. Retargeting also works on social media sites where a social media pixel stored on the user's machine can be used to target them with relevant advertisements once they leave a website. Google uses the word 'remarketing' to mean the ability to serve advertisements through the Google Display Network to anyone who visits a web page that has an audience tag. Bing calls this same concept remessaging.

There is a growing movement to phase out third-party cookies. First-party cookies are those that a website can store on its visitor's device. They have several advantages for UX and tracking within your web properties, and marketers use them to remember shopping carts, avoid re-logins and the like. However, third-party cookies are those that are stored on your visitor's device by a website other than your own, which are used to track the visitor's behaviour after they leave your website. These cookies are seen as snooping and a security threat and might be phased out soon, which is something that marketers need to keep in mind.

The advantage of using remarketing within Google's network of properties is that you can create your entire network of content on Google properties—content on websites that are crawled by Google and ranked for keywords, backlinks to this content from social media sites where your brand has a presence, which are tracked and used for domain authority calculations, and video content on YouTube, which is ranked for video searches and can also provide rich backlinks to your website. You can then build remarketing lists based on cookies stored on visitors' devices when they visit either your website or YouTube channel and remarket to them on Google Display Network. The only caveat is that you need more than 1,000 cookies for a remarketing audience to be created.

Retargeting can be done in two ways—directly by using the features of a particular platform like Google or Meta, for instance, or through a third-party programmatic service.

Using a third-party service gives you cross-platform access to more inventory. Inventory depends on the buyer persona of the SaaS product. For the most part, using platforms directly should work for SaaS marketers.

Other retargeting models have been used by companies that have their own advertisement networks. For instance, if a searcher types in a keyword and clicks on a result that takes the searcher to a website that belongs to this advertisement network, then they are served a retargeting advertisement based on their search query. Your prospects see advertisements on your products and offers with a very strong 'now' factor also incorporated that can nudge them to take action while they search. Sometimes, offers can be timed to create a sense of urgency like a 24-hour offer or one that lasts a few days, depending on the nature of the SaaS product.

Retargeting using social media has rapidly increased over the last ten years or so. The Meta family of social media, Facebook and Instagram, are very popular in this space. While the Google Display Network allows you to follow the user on a network of websites, social retargeting keeps your brand in front of the consumer in a more intimate space—the social network that they frequent. Searching for a technology solution and finding advertisements for it on your Facebook news feed or Instagram feed is not uncommon.

Intent retargeting, another form of retargeting, uses intent data to help SaaS marketers build more precise retargeting audiences based on their behaviour outside the marketer's asset base. We explored how intent data is captured when we looked at the shadow funnel. Tools like Demandbase not only give you intelligence on the nature and intention of visitors who frequent your website but also let you target audiences built on intent data matching your product category.

The logic behind using retargeting is pretty evident. You've done the hard work in getting a visitor to your website. If you can use other channels to further communicate messaging about your brand, you have a better chance of encouraging them through your marketing funnel. However, if you don't approach retargeting with the right strategy, it can be quite a costly experiment. Here are a few things to keep in mind while running retargeting campaigns.

Marketing funnels, in their most basic sense, start with an awareness stage, move to a consideration stage and then end with a decision. The stage at which you target someone should influence the channel you use and your advertising creative work. With most platforms, you can retarget visitors in great detail. Not only can you target those who have been on your website but also visitors that have viewed specific pages, which really helps to identify where visitors are in the funnel and, therefore, how you should interact with them. Here are some examples of how to target visitors at various stages.

You may think that you need not focus on the awareness stage with retargeting. If a visitor has already been on your website, naturally, they must know your brand. However, don't assume that this job is finished. There is likely still work to be done. You also do not want to start selling right away to someone who knows nothing about your brand or service. You need time to build trust and clearly communicate the value that you offer. For example, if somebody views a blog post, then consider retargeting them with a follow-on piece of content. Soon, visitors will start to associate your brand as being an expert in your chosen subject matter. Planting this seed is a great way to give visitors more confidence to consider your product/service in the future.

If visitors view specific features or products of yours, then you'll have an indication that they are in the consideration phase. In these instances, you can retarget them with specific messaging to ensure they continue to consider your product. Advertisements could focus on getting them to download a product guide or inviting them to sign up for a webinar about your product usage.

Again, you should not directly sell your product to them at this stage. You should take the opportunity to ensure that they move to the next stage of making a decision. A visitor viewing a pricing page is a pretty big indicator that they are close to making a decision on your product. What we've found to be particularly effective is using email to retarget visitors in real time.

If you can retarget in real time, you tap into an immediate interest in your brand. By including social proof, testimonials and rewards in the emails, we have seen open and click-through rates double in these retargeting campaigns when compared to other email marketing campaigns we've run. Another option here is to use proactive live-chat prompts, which can be tailored for each page and to individual visitors. This option provides a personalised experience considerate of the customer's customer journey and their past experiences with your brand.

Nurturing versus Retargeting

One of the greatest sales lines uttered on celluloid is the one from the movie *Glengarry Glen Ross*: 'ABC—Always Be Closing'.[3] In reality, closing a deal requires more than just a punch. SaaS deals need to be nurtured, not just retargeted to build recall. While retargeting keeps your brand relevant and in front of a prospect, nurturing is a more personalised way for a prospect to receive information about your offering. Nurturing primarily uses email but can also use other channels like messaging apps and physical media like desk drops.

Nurturing is not a new concept. Any good sales representative will tell you that customer relationships are built through careful nurturing, which makes closing deals easier. Lead nurturing in the traditional sense is about building a solid relationship with a prospect or customer. Now in SaaS, this needs to be done at scale. There could be 10, 100, 1,000 or 100,000 leads, and each of them must feel like this brand talks to 'me', like they know them and care about them. Traditionally, sales representatives would often share helpful content with the lead and generally stay in touch and learn more about them. Lead nurturing has the same three objectives—share relevant and useful content, stay in touch and, finally, learn more about a prospect to convert them to a customer.

If you look at a SaaS marketing funnel in a top-down manner, anyone who enters the funnel at the very top is not ready to make a buying decision. Your job as a SaaS marketer is to get as many of them interested as soon as possible, not by hammering them with pings and pongs but by nurturing them into believing that your brand is a credible source of information that solves their problems. They can start evaluating you for the same. The best part about lead nurturing is that it helps you stretch the cost per lead (CPL) you incur by a lot because the cost of nurturing, especially by email, is next to zero.

All top-performing SaaS companies use lead nurturing and attribute their success to it. Lead nurturing is a methodical, calculated approach that takes a customer on a journey that delivers real value to them to turn leads into paying customers at the forefront. Lead scoring plays a key role in nurturing leads and determining how the lead is progressing through the funnel. Scoring is like grading. A lead scoring system lets you assess how a lead has progressed towards actually purchasing your brand's products. Many leads do fall by the wayside and end up not being closed due to various factors, and that's okay. You simply need to sharpen your focus on the leads that are ready to engage with the sales team and continue communication with those that are not at a more relaxed pace.

Lead scoring is done based on several criteria. Consider a lead's demographic characteristics (industry, location, company size and the like) and behaviours (the number of click-throughs on your emails, form submissions, demonstrations or trial requests). Assign scored values to each behaviour, such as one point for an email click-through, five points for a free trial request and maybe three points for an e-book download. Totalling these points over time gives you a score. Setting a benchmark score for a lead becoming an MQL gives you a target. Here are a few criteria to consider for scoring:

1. Fit: Some leads will be a better fit than others for what you offer—alignment with target accounts, target industries and target personas.
2. Activity: Not all good-fit leads are active. How leads react to emails and whether they open emails, click links and read through, explore content, sign up for newsletters, watch webinars or download e-books can indicate buyer seriousness.
3. Interest: Not all who are active are interested. Look for specific cues such as time spent on site, followership on social media and engagement to estimate interest.
4. Buying Stage: Buying stage and time spent within the buying cycle can also indicate the likelihood of buying. Remember the SaaS marketing mantra—full life cycle engagement and pipeline acceleration. So even if the lead is in the sales pipeline, keep nurturing them.

Content plays a huge role in lead nurturing. Many marketers make the mistake of using the same content assets for different personas. One size doesn't fit all. Nurtures need to be created for personas, industries, stages of the funnel, products and buyer interest levels. Having a content factory in place that produces content for this nuanced segmentation is critical for the success of lead nurturing. Rather than bombarding personas with a slew of marketing messages, send them meaningful, targeted content that aligns with their needs, goals and interests. It could be a blog post that reflects something you spoke about or a webinar invitation that's targeted to a specific buyer persona.

Personalisation is another important aspect of lead nurturing. Many marketers confuse personalisation with just adding the lead's first name in the greeting! However, people prefer reading an email that was written with their context in mind and reads like it was written for them with a complete understanding of them. Personalisation is also driven by customer data platforms that capture all customer activity on the company's marketing assets. Personalised emails that are created or generated based on the lead's activity trail work best.

Having an omnichannel approach to lead nurturing is important. While we have been exploring the many virtues of email, social media channels like LinkedIn, where account-based targeting can be done, and messaging apps like WhatsApp, where most people are today, must also be considered. Open rates on WhatsApp messages are more than 98 per cent. So, the next time you wonder how to improve your email open rate from 20 per cent to 22 per cent, consider this!

Lead nurturing has many moving parts and does not work without a marketing automation platform. Marketo is the most popular choice, but there are also options like HubSpot and even CRM systems like Salesforce, which have built their marketing cloud. Automation of tasks like sending follow-up emails, sharing helpful content, scheduling calls or promoting events means less guesswork for the marketer and no chance of important events falling through the cracks. Automation systems also help provide analytics on nurture performance and lead progress and can point out the right moment when the lead is sales-ready.

Lead nurturing creates and maintains relationships with consumers at every stage of the purchasing process. Some of your potential leads may want to buy your brand's products and services immediately. Other leads may just be in their initial research-gathering phase. No matter where they are in their journey, you should make sure you connect with them by adding value, consistently and over time. In a world built on instant gratification, words like *consistent* and *over time* may seem anachronistic. However, successful lead nurturing will help you foster genuine, positive relationships with your customers. SaaS marketers should avoid impersonal, one-size-fits-all marketing that repulses customers.

Better lead nurturing has been proven to result in better relationships and more effective sales. Giving your leads the communication they *want* and *need* makes them far more likely to consider you than a competitor. By trying and experimenting and taking data-driven decisions, you can figure out what type and channel of communication work best for different types of leads. By trying out different types of lead nurturing strategies, you'll be able to see which types of leads connect most easily with your brand and understand which types of audiences to target on a larger scale.

Experimenting with different lead nurturing strategies is important because not every lead you encounter will be a good fit for your brand. Some leads you pursue may respond best to a certain style of communication, which is important to unearth. For instance, using WhatsApp to nurture leads who have filled out a contact form may work better than sending them a personalised email. Keeping an open and experimentative mind when it comes to lead nurturing is important.

We've touched upon content that a lead values. Creating this content depends on how well you understand problems that customers prioritise. How can you solve their problem and solve it better than anyone else? Where does your brand fit into their needs? Figure out your best qualifications for each lead, and be prepared to sell them on your answers. A generic pitch may give you some results in a 'spray and pray' approach, but a personalised approach is needed.

Choosing the right channel for nurturing is also important. Some leads may be active on social media. Others may prefer email campaigns. Determine their patterns and preferences by testing different channel nurtures and finding the ones that they respond to well. Communication is much easier when it's through someone's preferred channel and can result in a good response rate and faster movement through the pipeline.

SaaS marketers can use several channels for lead nurturing, and all of them have their pros and cons. Email works well as mentioned earlier. It's a quick, reliable way to engage with leads and keep their attention. However, there are some cautionary tales when it comes to email. Make emails user-friendly and easy to understand and navigate. Text with embedded links works beautifully. Don't be tempted by image-heavy emails that your mail server will block anyway. No matter what kind of content you have, a difficult-to-parse email turns off readers. Offering helpful information with relevant embedded links is golden.

Adding cross-links to websites, social handles and key news updates like recent funding or acquisitions helps to build the image and makes you stand out. Personalised emails are worth doing or else don't do emails. Tailor your emails to specific leads and their problems, industry, personas, recent activity and so on. Let them know that you're putting in an effort to know them. It's like making a friend!

Avoid overloading leads with emails. Sending an email once a week is good, but twice may be a stretch. Anything more than that is a disaster waiting for the unsubscribe button to happen. Relentless emailing gets you ignored, blocked and/or, more importantly, taken off the buyer's consideration set of potential providers. Despite pressure from demand generation teams to accelerate leads through the email pipeline to generate more MQLs, be the voice of reason that espouses steady, relevant, value-adding communication. Avoid being pushy or negative. Even if a lead is not where you want them to be in the sales process, keep communicating with them at a comfortable pace. Friendships are not made at gunpoint!

Social media works very well for nurturing leads as well. Using social media retargeting ads as part of a workflow can keep relevant content in front of the eyes of the lead in areas where they 'have their guard down', so to speak. Making website content dynamic by detecting the presence of the lead so that they get served information and recommendations based on past browsing behaviour is possible. This method works for leads who are just beginning to gather preliminary information about you.

Using social media requires creating a wide variety of content types. Explore what kinds of content your leads like and respond to, be it videos, blog posts or snappy tweets. Create content that's different from your email campaigns. Use new tone, style and copy, especially on social media. Brand voices should vary across channels, but the essence should be retained. Interacting with prospect accounts and buyer personas on social media platforms is a proven tactic. Go ahead and like that pearl of wisdom your prospect just dropped in their LinkedIn post. Replying to their social media posts, answering queries and following their accounts and asking to be followed go a long way to forming a genuine relationship with leads.

On the flip side, social media can seduce you into being cool without substance. Memes, GIFs and funky designs are cool, but keep the end goal in mind for your content, even on social media platforms. Avoid negative comments or reactions towards customers and prospects, even if they comment harshly on one of your posts. If you get negative feedback, try to 'prove them wrong'. Handle complaints from leads with grace.

Using marketing automation wisely is also important. If a lead is someone who has just shown a hint of interest, do not use your automation tool to bombard them with twenty emails in two weeks. Let their curiosity build with TOFU assets and then lead them further into the S&M pipeline. Aim for quality, repeatability and consistency. Sending an insight-filled email at the same time each week will create an imprint and make your brand recognisable and may even foster an expectation of content.

Going off the automation tool to manually nurture critical leads is also fine. For instance, if your SaaS company wants to acquire unicorn companies as customers, that's a finite set of maybe a hundred companies in India. Relying on automation in those cases might not be the best solution.

Create a customised email that can go to them from the desk of your chief executive officer (CEO) or even your chief marketing officer (CMO). A customised approach keeps your nurturing strategy nimble enough to deal with custom requests and needs. Use automation, but don't become an automaton. Build real human customer relationships.

Email is dead. Long live email. According to Statista, global email users will grow from 3.7 billion last year to more than 4.2 billion by 2022. Over 333 billion emails are sent in a day. Per ThinData, 80 per cent of marketers agree that email marketing is one of the most effective strategies. Most business buyers check their email every day. You own your opt-in list. You can reach out to your followers on any social media platform. The platform is certainly here to stay for the foreseeable future.

The solution to the problem of people getting too much email is to make sure that you send emails that they bookmark or want to read while ignoring the 99 per cent that they don't want to. If your content is valuable, your prospect will want to get your emails. So you can dodge bullets like 'email is dead' or 'too many emails'.

Your 'money pages' must be kept in mind while nurturing and retargeting. Money pages contain the core of your product and offer information and value propositions from which a prospect can convert to a customer. Keeping the website the centrepiece of this activity helps you do so. Emails must be optimised to be mobile-first. Instead of putting the full article in the email, show a part of it and get the leads to click through to land on a blog or a website-hosted page. Then there should be a paragraph or two that draws them in even further. Follow that up with a call to action (CTA) that links them back to the full article on your website.

According to Statista, 54 per cent of global website traffic comes from mobile devices. Using device-based testing tools already provided in marketing automation platforms, emails can be tested and optimised for a variety of devices such as mobile phones and tablets. Both your website and your emails need to be mobile-ready, especially in a B2B context. If you use tools like HubSpot or Marketo or even Mailchimp, these features are in-built.

Other aspects of emails must also be tested such as what the overall email looks like, what the subject line is like and what the opening image looks like. Subject lines are important because having the right subject line can tell the reader whether an email is meaningful or spam. There is always a temptation to add the core of the content in the subject line like offers, discounts, free trials and so on. These tend to get customers' backs up and lead to lower open rates because B2B SaaS customers do not open emails expecting offers. They expect value and good content. Subject lines should interest people and pull them into the content. Just making minor changes to the subject line can increase your open rate.

The right balance in sending emails is where you get enough value for your content and don't drive up unsubscribe rates. If you do a reasonably good job of getting a 25–30 per cent open rate and see some good engagement with the click-throughs, then you need to increase your frequency of sending. You should learn from every single campaign you send. So, follow the data. Look at how your audience reacts to each email and then use that data in a variety of ways. While measuring email nurture performance, open rates are vanity and click-through rates are reality. It shows you the engagement you create. Using the right URL structure, you can track their activity and then interlink all of your content from the one landing page to drive more relevant content and get the prospect in a deep dive mode. Use it to make the subsequent campaigns even better. Use it as a guide for how to segment your audience or as a way to determine the frequency of your campaigns.

Lead nurturing with messaging is a new concept that has come to light with the consumer adoption of messaging apps. Over 175 million people around the world message a business account on WhatsApp, and over 90 per cent of Instagram users follow a business on Instagram. WhatsApp has message open rates of 98 per cent and can be a credible channel for lead nurturing. Messaging apps are more intimate spaces as compared to emails and can get better response rates and two-way communication with your SaaS brand as compared to emails and retargeting via banner ads.

The key to using messaging for nurturing is automation. Just like marketing automation platforms are used to automate emails, conversational engagement platforms are used to automate two-way conversations between brands and customers. To a limited extent, Short Message Service (SMS) is being used by e-commerce companies to remind consumers to complete their check out after adding products to the cart or to inform them of transaction and delivery details. However, it's hard to reply to an SMS sent by a business, at least in India. Two-way conversations are not possible. The main messaging channel to use is WhatsApp.

In today's fast-paced world, your prospects find it very convenient to communicate with you via WhatsApp as most people have some sort of smartphone or tablet with them at all times. Like email, your prospects must opt-in before you can send them WhatsApp messages. WhatsApp provides templates that it approves. Working with a business solutions provider (BSP) of WhatsApp is the best way to get started. Opt-ins can be obtained via WhatsApp messages, text messages, emails or voice calls. You shouldn't buy mobile numbers and cold-spam people to get opt-in.

Build a nurture journey that has not only the key content items that you want to send the prospect but also the responses that you want your chatbot to give if the prospect has questions about the content you shared. Writing for messaging is a skill in itself because it requires brevity. 'Keep it shorter' is the mantra here, shorter than email. Message timing is also important like timing emails is. Studying open rates against the time of day and week will help to identify the right time to send messages.

If done correctly, nurturing with messaging can be done more frequently. As consumers, your customers are used to getting messages from banks, credit card companies and e-commerce companies daily, telling them about a variety of things ranging from their bank balance to order confirmations and delivery schedules. The messages are not intrusive to them if they have signed up for it or have a familiarity with it. Similar to email nurturing, it is important to not brag but to share assets and important information that adds value to your prospects. Pre-creating chatbot sequences that can engage with prospects across a variety of assets is important.

Also, the customer engagement platform you choose needs to be integrated with the CRM system you use and the marketing automation system, among others, so that a true omnichannel engagement model can be created that combines email with messaging, retargeting and other channels of engagement. There are no true stand-alone software systems that work but a combined effort that works best.

WhatsApp is not just a person-to-person (P2P) messaging tool. Thanks to services such as WhatsApp Business, using WhatsApp for marketing is possible. Today, consumers rely on phones to handle everyday tasks. People waiting in line or commuting check their to-do list for the day, read mails, answer work-related messages on Slack or other collaboration tools or just scroll through social media. WhatsApp is, by far, the most popular global messaging channel. It has a staggering 2 billion monthly active users—significantly more than any other app on the market, with Instagram and WeChat in China coming close. People all over the planet use it to easily connect with family and friends through smartphones, laptops, desktop computers, tablets and even smartwatches, especially in mobile-first countries.

With the consumer adoption of WhatsApp at its peak, Meta started to open their WhatsApp to brands. As mentioned earlier, 175 million people message a business on WhatsApp daily. What has helped is that WhatsApp has taken care to protect users and left it up to them to decide whether or not they wish to talk to a business via WhatsApp or not. You can see this in the block/opt-out button you see when you receive communications from a business on WhatsApp. Most people opt-in and let businesses talk to them. They feel safe and comfortable because it is a place where they already are. They trust the app immensely.

In the traditional sales processes, you had a phone number and phone calls were one of the great ways to establish a relationship with a client. Calling was replaced by emails and they became commonplace. As time passed, both channels reached their peak. Cold emailing is a dying tactic. Tools were developed to block unwanted calls and emails. WhatsApp can be an effective way to not make customers uncomfortable. More than five million businesses use WhatsApp business accounts. According to App Annie, on average, WhatsApp users (on the Android platform) spend 19.4 hours per month (38 minutes per day) using the app. Businesses can tap into this attention zone that customers already have. The process of engaging with consumers is through conversations and not through bulk messages, cold calls and emails.

WhatsApp also limits how its API is used. Online games and gambling companies are not allowed to use it. Message templates are screened strictly to make sure that the platform is not abused and that active users of WhatsApp are not turned away because businesses are misusing it. Therefore, businesses rethink the way they approach and communicate with customers.

WhatsApp is preferred over SMS by businesses for its ability to foster two-way conversations. WhatsApp belongs to the category of messaging channels called IP messaging. They operate on data—either mobile data or Wi-Fi—and do not need any carrier to support them, unlike SMS. WhatsApp can be accessed on any device, while SMSs are limited to mobile phone usage. WhatsApp can be used to chat, do voice calls and exchange rich media content with anyone across the world for free. So, a company that needs to send SMSs to multiple prospects and customers across the world is caught in a global web of tariffs controlled by mobile carriers and other aggregators. WhatsApp messages bypass SMS roaming fees or fluctuating carrier costs because they're delivered as an over-the-top (OTT) messaging platform, making it ideal for a client base in different regions. SMSs have their advantages too. They can be sent to any mobile device, but WhatsApp can only be sent to devices that have the app installed.

Instead of using more traditional calling and email methods, WhatsApp allows video calling, exchange of videos and voice messages. A marketer can send demonstrations, an inside sales team can send communications and a sales representative can send quotes and proposals. WhatsApp allows for asynchronous communication, meaning the customer can reply at their convenience and the chatbot continues the conversation. WhatsApp messages are seen within minutes of delivery.

Just like every business creates a Google business profile for better searchability, every SaaS business must create a WhatsApp account. It's an opportunity to communicate your brand history and positioning and link all your brand elements into your WhatsApp conversations. You can add contact numbers, website URLs, office locations, free trial details, demonstration days, promotional details, product recommendations and more. Also, WhatsApp's end-to-end encryption feature makes these conversations private between businesses and users.

Calls, emails and SMSs will continue to be used even by SaaS businesses, but they will co-exist with more modern forms of lead nurturing. They have their place. Messaging apps like WhatsApp, however, allow you to forge a deeper connection with your consumers in the same way that digital marketing gives you scale, cost-effectiveness and flexibility.

Nurturing with Chatbots and Conversational AI

In the previous section, we saw how WhatsApp can be an effective channel for lead nurturing using chatbots. AI-based chatbots are SaaS marketers' modern friends for customer engagement. Chatbots can power lead generation, enhance customer journeys and help you nurture leads into conversation qualified leads (CQLs). Chatbots can be simple structured bots and also use technologies like AI, natural language programming and speech recognition. AI-powered chatbots can help you in conversational marketing. Conversational marketing is based on three factors—how you capture customer intent, how you deliver personalised experiences and how you engage through the life cycle of the customer.

Let's discover how chatbots merge conversational excellence with intelligent AI algorithms to nurture leads! The most important aspect of chatbot-based lead nurturing is customer segmentation. Nurturing your leads needs segmentation of customers, which will help you to personalise the content as per the segment of the customer. Segmentation needs data collection, aggregation and analysis to create segments of buyers that even the marketer may not have thought of.

Chatbots can extract data from conversations with various users, aggregate them, merge them into a master data catalogue, enrich them through third-party data sources and then make the data ready for further analysis. For instance, a chatbot may capture five fields (name, designation, company, mobile number and email ID) but then would need to enrich the data by adding fields of company industry, revenue, size, employees, head office and so on, which can all be done programmatically.

Once that is done, segmentation algorithms can create segments based on demography, psychography, geography and behavioural changes, based on interactions of users, the questions they ask and the use cases that they look for while interacting with the chatbot. Once this approach is used to define the target personas, identify the differentiator for each, design chatbot interactions that leverage data collected about each persona, keep collecting more data based on fresh interactions and, via the bot automation platform, offer recommendations to resolve customer queries.

Every interaction between a customer and your business does not qualify for a lead, but identifying a lead from several interactions is also not easy. Chatbots can leverage AI-based technologies to identify specific patterns to segregate leads.

For example, if you are looking to find leads for your SaaS business, you need to segregate between leads that can be an enterprise company or a mid-market company or a small and midsize business (SMB) with an interest in your product services. Identifying these leads and getting to know their intent is key to figuring out the conversational experience the bot is offering them.

One of the most conventional approaches that marketers used for data collection was forms. Customers would fill details in the form on a landing page that marketing teams then leverage for lead identification and segregation. Filling out a form adds friction to the lead flow process, and customers would much rather not fill out a voluminous form or fill out just one field like email ID and leave it at that. Non-serious prospects won't even fill in their official ID.

Here, a chatbot can help you collect data without a form. Chatbots can extract a lot of data from prospects by keeping them engaged in a two-way conversation. A chatbot can help you gather data for lead generation and gather crucial information to nurture the lead up to the point of sale or at least up to the point of marketing qualification till the sales team can take over.

Chatbots are considered one of the most effective marketing tools for user engagement. The reason is simple—these AI-based tools offer chat personalisation. Organisations can enable personalised recommendations and specific services and even suggest solutions to customers through chatbots. Businesses can integrate chatbots into their CRM systems to enhance personalisation. So, ignoring the personalisation aspect of marketing is not an option. Some of the best CRM tools that can help in chatbot integration are Salesforce, Zoho CRM, HubSpot CRM and Zendesk to name a few.

The AI-based way to capture and nurture your leads involves the following:

1. Offering chatbots to visitors at applicable times on websites and landing pages
2. Asking the visitors who engage for their email and some qualifying questions
3. Learning more about the lead through data appends (CRM, social, other)
4. Passing the visitors to the next step in the process—whether a human representative, an email capture (so the bot can send interesting content) or something else
5. Switching on your lead nurturing and conversion machine (of which content marketing is usually a key part)

This new process doesn't mean that humans are never in the loop, just that they're handed more qualified and informed leads, which are then easier to convert. Messaging will be the prime communication mode in the future. Super-speedy chatbots put the 'instant' in instant messaging. The best chatbots include the ability to add someone else (for example, from your Slack contacts list) to a conversation, auto-email conversations after a period of inactivity (for example, 15 minutes), infer intent from complex language and deliver conversational replies, and offer proactive chat at places in the experience known to have higher engagement.

The best chatbots integrate with calendar and conferencing apps such as Calendly, Assistant.to and Zoom so that, at the appropriate time in the chat experience, your bot can send a call scheduling link to the visitor. Best of all, it frees you and your administrative staff to do more valuable work. The leading chatbots offer API-level integrations with your customer-facing apps, such as Google Calendar for scheduling meetings, CRMs for visibility into customer contact activity, marketing automation suites like HubSpot and Marketo, social media accounts (through data appends, explained later), e-commerce stores like Shopify to access transactional data and knowledge bases to quickly refer prospects to useful articles. For example, by integrating with a CRM app like Salesforce, SugarCRM or Zendesk, your chatbot can directly pull customer and prospect data into your sales representative's workspace.

Using only the email entered, capable chatbot platforms can leverage third-party apps to append data such as full name, location, job title, company information and links to social profiles. Some data append vendors even offer predictive models and lead scoring algorithms, which help you prioritise the leads with which your chatbot should engage. Even better, they can do this in real time. Together with the transactional data fed in from your CRM, these tie-ins give your representatives a more well-rounded picture of your prospects, which helps to build rapport and increase close rates.

Perhaps the coolest feature of the latest chatbots is their ability to do semantic analysis, that is, to deduce the visitor's intent based on words and phrases used in the current and previous conversations. This 'thinking' part of the AI algorithms used in chatbots is what makes them 'relational concierges' in the sales process.

Chatbots can calculate a meaningful connection score (MCS) as early as possible in the discussion with each visitor. Each message sent by a visitor is analysed in real time and gets a positive or negative score. The scores are continuously combined to determine the emotional content of the conversation, resulting in an 'overall MCS' at the end of each discussion. A higher MCS score means that the lead is more interested in what you're selling. The main point of your interactions with prospects is to generate more qualified leads. By asking qualifying questions tailored to your solution context and prospect personas—like 'Which of these situations best describes you?' (prospect persona), 'How large is your company?' and 'How soon are you looking to purchase a [XYZ] solution?'—and tailoring the follow-up messaging accordingly, these apps let visitors self-select whether they're a good fit for a given product. By doing so, they avoid wasting everyone's (representatives', account executives' and prospects') time and they build trust. Don't you respect someone more when they determine they're not the best solution for you and even refer you to another vendor?

Some platforms allow you to choose a persona or online personality for your chatbot that includes the right mix of personality attributes like directness, empathy, helpfulness and persuasiveness. Conversational designers can work with SaaS marketers to develop that. For example, an e-commerce store could configure its customer service representative to have a persona with more empathy and helpfulness. A SaaS seller, on the other hand, might configure their account executive bot to be more direct and persuasive. In addition, most chatbot apps for paid subscriptions allow you to customise your chatbot's visual 'look and feel' and branding (including adding your company logo). Since every chat is a touchpoint in your customer's journey, every impression matters.

The Industry of Content

Everything that we have discussed in the previous sections is dependent on content. Today, content is king and can help engage with a prospect and create a positive (or negative) brand image. Earlier, content writing was considered a non-core part of marketing, relegated to writing emails, brochures or website copy. Today, it is at the tip of any marketing incision a SaaS marketer wants to make. Three factors have driven the content revolution, especially for SaaS—the rise of search, search engine optimisation (SEO) and social media. Content is key to driving the discoverability of a SaaS brand, building credibility for the brand in the eyes of the buyer personas and users and nurturing and maintaining relationships with customers across the life cycle.

The last twenty years of content marketing have been defined by the integration between multichannel marketing, social media and SEO. Facebook, Twitter, LinkedIn, Instagram, YouTube and many others have become the primary channels through which brands reach their customers. This development has led to both strategic and tactical approaches to content creation and distribution. SaaS brands adapt their content for different channels. At the same time, they became more flexible and differentiated in their approaches to content creation to differentiate themselves from competitors.

Google popularised the hero-hub-hygiene model for YouTube content publishers, which is now being used across the board by companies. The framework helps companies to differentiate between types of content, objectives and frequencies of publishing. Hero content builds high-level messaging and establishes authority. This type of content usually aligns with a brand campaign. For instance, a brand manifesto video is a hero asset, which talks about the brand's reason to exist and its vision of the world. The video can be accompanied by written material in the form of blogs, web page content, social media campaigns and so on. Hub content is regularly scheduled push content that supports the theme of the hero campaign and is designed to create a 'double click' level of awareness.

In the brand manifesto example, hygiene content can be a series of videos, e-books or blogs on the solutions categories underlying the brand umbrella. Hygiene content is typically content that people search for. This type of content is more oriented to practicality, such as how-tos, three things to keep in mind, five steps to achieve an objective and so on.

This framework can also be married to TOFU, MOFU and BOFU to create an effective interlock. The TOFU content seeks to educate and attract and can sit across the hero, hub and hygiene types. The MOFU content seeks to engage and add more detail and can map to the hub and hygiene content types, and the BOFU content seeks to convince and usually maps to the hygiene content type.

The other major trend that's emerged in the last twenty years is the rise of SEO. Blogs made it possible for anyone and everyone to be a publisher, including brands themselves. However, with the rise of Google in the early 2000s, marketers began realising that for people to find their blog content, they needed to make it appear at the top of Google search engine results pages. Search has spawned an entire industry of people who build backlinks and perform outreach for the sole purpose of getting pieces of content to rank. Market segmentation and customer roadmaps have also led to a proliferation of content marketing formats. Outside of blog posts, many brands also invest in the creation of e-books, whitepapers, reports, testimonials, case studies, sell sheets and videos. Some brands today have content marketing down to a science—knowing exactly what types of content to serve customers to get them to take the desired action. They then use content intelligence software to measure the exact impact their content has and adjust their strategy accordingly.

The internet exploded in the 1990s. A lot of marketing focus moved from print and television to digital media, and millions of websites proliferated, leading to the creation of the generation of bloggers mentioned earlier. Email was born, both corporate and personal, and e-commerce started, which laid the foundation for web-based businesses to take birth. In the 2000s, social networks such as Twitter, Facebook, LinkedIn and YouTube also came up, which provided new platforms for content creations to publish and for brands to find their audience on each of these platforms.

In the last few years, user-created content has exploded, and brands have made their users and customers the heroes and the creators of content that others can value.

4

Onboarding in the Era of Customer Success

Customer Support to Customer Success

Customer success is a programme that helps your customers achieve value with your SaaS product or service, rather than momentary satisfaction. Over the years, it has become a structured practice and combines a relationship-based, proactive approach with tools and programmatic means to help customers achieve maximum value from their SaaS investments. In simple terms, customer success is about making sure your customers are successful so that you can be successful. However, customer service/support and customer success are not the same, though they are commonly confused. Customer service is focused on solving customer problems before, during and after purchase. Customer support is a reactive and more problem-based approach that aims to be there for a customer for anything that they need. Customer success, on the other hand, is a proactive, relationship-focused and holistic approach to making SaaS customers successful with their investment. Customer service and support are largely measured through levels of CSAT, but customer success is measured in terms of usage, renewals, NPS and a host of other parameters.

Customer success is the most important function in a SaaS business because it becomes the means to retain and expand customers once they are acquired. A SaaS business is built on new, renew and expand motions, and renew is one of the key motions that customer success aims for and is responsible for. Any renewal rate below 95 to 98 per cent in SaaS is considered unacceptable, and customer success plays a key role in ensuring that the rate does not drop. The other goal of customer success is to create more customers from existing customers—making the retained customers so happy with your product that they start talking about your product with their peers and industry. Word of mouth is a key driver of organic inbound enquiries into the business, and customer success can enable that.

One of the hottest roles in the SaaS market is that of the CSM. A CSM is responsible for onboarding a SaaS customer's users, training them as needed, creating an environment for them to start using the service, tracking and monitoring usage and, finally, leveraging all of this to drive renewals. By looking into customer data and feedback, CSMs seek to understand customer usage trends and challenges proactively, even before they become trends that customers can spot.

SaaS marketing partners closely with the customer success team, and this is referred to as customer marketing or retention marketing—an intersection of product, marketing and customer success. Just like product marketers work with product management teams, customer marketers work with CSMs to successfully onboard, drive usage and ensure retention. Customer marketers also help to maintain a consistent CX throughout the life cycle. Onboarding material, user guides, product documentation, product emailers and usage contests are developed and delivered to customers in a targeted manner at scale. Customer marketers work to ensure that customers see value in the product, renew or purchase from the company again and advocate the product to their network.

Customer marketers own content such as onboarding materials, presentations, email nurture tracks, product communications, feature highlights, customer events, webinars and case studies. Customer marketers can also report to the chief customer officer or vice president (VP) of the customer success function, depending on the company's organisational structure, but can also live in the CMO organisation. Customer marketers need to stay tightly connected with the triad and quad to ensure a consistent CX.

Ideal customer marketers need to be customer-centric—the customer must be at the centre of every decision marketers make. They bring in the customer perspective in all internal discussions. Always be 'outside-in' when the rest of your company is 'inside-out'. Empathy is a key capability because there is a need to listen to customer challenges, issues and even feedback and channel that positively into the company's product and go-to-market programmes. Being a team player is extremely important when you are working in a triad or a quad. Customer marketers cannot pull the team in one direction without getting the buy-in from the others. They also need to possess the skills to speak the language of product, customer success and sales, apart from marketing. Customer marketers must also be good narrators of product capability because that needs to come out in all the materials and nudges that they create for the end user.

Having a customer marketer in your marketing organisation is not enough. The customer marketing team needs to be aligned with the customer success team. For starters, marketing should be measured on customer success outcomes like net retention rate and NPS. Also, other metrics that cover crucial phases like onboarding are important for marketers to co-own the onboarding process with the customer success teams. If a hundred accounts are closed by sales but twenty leave during the onboarding phase due to difficulty and challenges, then that doesn't augur well for the business. Also, a SaaS company needs a customer marketing team only if the scale of operation merits one. If you onboard a handful of customers every month, you don't need one. You'd rather build a team that drives demand and gets more customers into the pipeline. However, if you have achieved lead momentum and scale in customer growth, then keep a portion of the marketing team focused purely on demand and split the marketing team into a lead generation-focused team and a customer marketing team.

Other customer-focused metrics that marketing can be measured on are usage, product adoption and customer expansion. Jointly renewing churn and renewals can help marketers and CSMs focus on the right set of customer accounts that need attention. Analysis of common pain points can provide insights into needs that are not being met. Some cancellations are due to factors beyond your control like lack of budget, but the ones that cancel due to value not being realised are worth their weight in gold for the insight that they give you if you wear the right lens.

Apart from NPSs, which are collected in-product or via a variety of channels like email or call, conducting sentiment analysis on social media is something the customer marketer can do. Given the product is B2B, looking at enterprise review sites like G2 and Gartner Peer Insights will help the marketer get a sense of how customers review your SaaS product on a third-party site, like using Tripadvisor for SaaS!

Also, with NPS, customer marketers can identify promoters and detractors and work on mitigation strategies. Once you get this kind of data, looking at patterns is important. Are there certain personas that are more critical than others? Are there certain verticals where feedback is usually good and verticals where it is usually middling or bad? Look at other patterns like age groups that can give you insight that you might normally miss.

Customer marketers should also focus on the following metrics along with the customer success team. Usage metrics tell us how the usage of a particular part of your product or a certain set of products is correlated with retention metrics. The marketing team can play an important role in improving usage with customised and timely nudges delivered across multiple channels. Customer activation and onboarding have their own set of metrics that indicate how many user licences have been activated and used and how the initial usage is trending. Campaigns to get usage started can be conceptualised by the customer marketing team working with the CSM.

The onboarding experience is the most dynamic part of the life cycle that needs to be customised for different account types, user groups, geographies and verticals. Identifying which actions customers took during successful onboarding processes is good to record to redesign your onboarding around that. Typically, onboarding does not start until customers have started using or consuming, depending on the type of SaaS business model you follow. Have your customer marketing team create nurturing campaigns that instruct customers how to step through the repeatable parts of your onboarding process. Save your customer team's time for more complicated issues like overall strategy or custom implementations.

Once the customer is onboarded and has started using the service, expansion metrics need to come into focus such as identifying customers who are ready to be cross-sold or upsold. Customer marketers can leverage usage data to identify triggers that are key indicators of when a customer is ready for either a new feature or an upsell to a higher category of usage more premium than what they currently use. Once identified, depending on the type and size of the customer, the right channel and methodology of communication is used—sales team, in-product message, email, WhatsApp message and the like.

SaaS marketing teams can also be split the way sales teams are. Just like there are hunters and farmers in the sales teams, marketing can also have demand generation marketers that bring in new leads and marketers that focus on extracting maximum revenue and delivering maximum impact to accounts that have closed. Thus, customer marketing teams can be measured on generating customer leads by identifying the nudge events for cross-sell, upsell, expansion and renewals. They can also be measured in driving successful onboarding of customers who have just been signed by using a combination of documentation, nurture sequences, onboarding campaigns and customer journeys.

Customer marketers can also be the voice of the company, owning all customer communications in the form of newsletters, product updates, outage announcements, event communications and so on. They can also be measured on how they turn customers into champions through positive word of mouth. They can run campaigns to get heavy users of the product to provide positive reviews on G2, Gartner Peer Insights and other third-party review sites and also recruit them for referral calls with prospective customers and even investors. Case studies make the best lead generation assets, and getting customers to provide approvals for case studies can be a key responsibility area (KRA) of a customer marketer.

One of the biggest factors helping this movement of customer success and customer marketing is the evolution of the customer. As we saw in the previous section, buyers have moved away from the 'buy it for me' mindset to a user mindset where they want to use, test for a fit and then buy. This mindset creates fertile ground for them to be educated, nurtured, helped, guided and prodded. SaaS buyers want to help themselves, and customer marketers and CSMs help them to help themselves. In this case, let's take a self-service experience. If you help the product team identify common, repeatable tasks that can be done via self-service, then you free up time to focus on more unique customer scenarios and use cases.

If you help to build a knowledge base by interviewing and polling your customer success and support teams to identify the most commonly asked questions, you can build a robust FAQ library, which can start as one page but can grow into a complete knowledge repository that is searchable and covers more areas of your product/service. Eventually, once you get to a critical mass of customers, they can also help each other through participation in forums and communities where questions and issues can be raised and answered by the group members. Building a community also fosters the feeling of a tribe around your SaaS brand and saves manual effort expended in support.

Customer Marketing in Self-Service

Thinking of the customer success and customer marketing teams in self-service motions is probably counter-intuitive, but incorporating them is beneficial. A virtual customer success environment can be created within the self-service experience so that all of your customers feel supported even when they decide to help themselves instead of seeking the help of an enterprise customer success team.

The self-service experience should be designed to support customers depending on the type of support they need and also the type of reference format they prefer. Some may prefer reading through the documentation, while others may prefer watching a video. Some prefer that the product itself guides them while they use it, and others need none of these—they want to do it purely on their own! You need to be consistent in the content you provide and be supportive in all these different formats at the same time. The goal is to create those moments in their usage journey where they feel that they can use this product, achieve success with it and depend on it.

Guided tours are quite popular in self-service experiences. For this, the first few starter features that the customer might use to move into your product need to be determined. You can understand this by subjecting your self-service experience in the staging environment to a small or large test group. Once the starter features are identified, they become the essence of the onboarding experience. From there on, users need to be guided deeper into the experience. Some of these common features, depending on the type of service you provide, could be creating an account, creating a test campaign, uploading a list and so on. However, do not rely on intuition and testing alone. Keep tracking usage data and determine additional insights. By understanding user patterns, the starter feature list and the experience can be changed so that the first experience, the onboarding experience, is successful and leads to bigger and better things.

If your service includes a multiple-step process, then adding a progress bar is a great way to move users across different phases and give them a sense of accomplishment as they do. Mailchimp has a progress bar in its self-service experience, as the user was guided across the various stages of setting up and executing an email campaign. This feature helps in two ways—the customer feels like they are on a journey and they are being guided through it via the progress bar. In addition to providing a sense of accomplishment, progress can also be fun. Adding some humour also helps, provided it aligns with your brand voice. Progress bars give confidence to users and inspire them to use the product more.

Just like sales teams need marketing support to deliver, customer success teams need customer marketing teams to help customers for whom they cannot provide dedicated support. The customer marketing team, as discussed earlier, makes sure customers are always involved and learning about your service by engaging them with different formats of self-service resources. Instead of scaling an in-person CSM team to design and execute the onboarding communications and ongoing marketing communications, integrate these assets into the self-service experience. Make sure that the customer gets information and nudges through emails and other channels even when they are out of the experience.

Each CSM (and, by extension, customer marketing) communication focuses on the onboarding steps of the customer journey. These steps are built into documentation or communicated via on-demand videos. Engagement can be increased with 'how to' articles and videos. Content on market leadership can be injected. Users can also share insights on where they fit vis-a-vis their peer group that also uses your platform. Sharing insights gained from other customers, surveys and reports is also a great way of giving customers a feel of customer success without having a dedicated person.

In-app guidance is a great way to create nudges for users within your product experience. In-app guidance can be used to create a good onboarding experience. In addition, it can be used to nudge users to try new features, upgrade them to a higher-level plan based on their usage of the product and move them into an enterprise sales relationship if their usage so merits. Building a knowledge base is essential to delivering an effective self-service experience. Given the nature of content consumption these days, creating micro-learning assets is important to give users information and insight. These assets should provide specific information. Also, information architecture can be created that uses a topic hierarchy and then links it to assets of different formats so that users can choose the format they want. Curated journeys can be created to guide them through the learning process.

With the growth of edtech and online education, in the last ten years, users have become accustomed to different modes of learning. Some like to learn sequentially, some like to learn and relearn until they understand the concept and others prefer micro-learning where they go into the knowledge base and get an answer to their questions. Marketers must also update the knowledge base continuously as the product evolves and based on feedback received from users.

Combining in-person training with virtual training is possible with webinars. Webinars are powerful because they can influence better onboarding and more usage in an on-demand format. They live on as thought leadership content that users can go back to. They also become discoverable via organic search, especially if they are uploaded on YouTube and other video hosting platforms with backlinks to your brand's website. Some users still prefer to learn from a live teacher. The attraction is in the ability to ask and handle questions. The way to solve this issue for recorded webinars is to leverage the simu-live (simulated live) model where the webinar runs in a recorded manner and an expert is present for the last 10 minutes to answer questions.

Webinars can be held in a variety of ways depending on where your users are geographically. Some companies run weekly webinars early in the mornings Pacific time, which covers most time zones except the far eastern ones, while others prefer early morning Eastern time to accommodate late times in the Far East and most of Asia and Europe. Holding live webinars periodically is recommended so that the active participation of users can be encouraged, and companies do this weekly, fortnightly or monthly.

A great way to strengthen user relationships is to also get them to participate in these webinars as guests and even as hosts so that it is truly user-generated knowledge. The CSM or customer marketer can be a co-host. Users talking about how the SaaS solution has helped them are the biggest hits because they give maximum confidence to others to try out the solution. Popular webinars where attendees ask relevant questions that can help others can be saved in an on-demand format and can also be repurposed into other formats like blogs.

Customer participation also creates a virtuous cycle and an aspirational quotient for more customers to want to be a part of the webinar in future. It makes the content more interesting, leads to more engagement and so on. Your SaaS brand comes across as a thought leader that has the support of industry experts who want to be seen as innovators and thought leaders.

While all these elements bring in the customer success experience at scale to self-service users, CSMs are freed to focus more on high-value accounts and engage with them in meaningful ways. The self-service portal takes care of the bulk of users who work themselves into high-value accounts. CSMs can also focus on elevating relevant self-service users into enterprise plans. All this is possible if their focus is kept on value accounts instead of any account that has a question.

The other aspect that helps CSMs is a vibrant community. We touched upon this briefly. It is common knowledge that prospects and customers like to connect with each other and learn from each other. They want to share their challenges and find solutions that they can try. They are often on the lookout for early adopters of new ideas and technology so that they, as the early majority or late majority or laggards, can do the same. Users connect to learn from each other, and they value this kind of learning more than what they can get from your knowledge base or conversation with a CSM. A community around your brand can enable all of this.

As a customer marketer, you need to define the objectives of creating the community. If you feel the objective is to answer questions, then that's fine too. Other objectives for communities include driving engagement, generating new ideas, finding new customers and getting feedback on products. Metrics can be created for each objective. Ownership of community building should not rest with the customer marketer or CSM but should move into the realm of developer relations (DevRel) if your product is used by developers or community management if it is a community of users that you want to build.

Irrespective of whether you hire for DevRel or community management functions, they will oversee the growth of the community and be the liaison between your product and business teams and the users out there. Community builders typically sit in product or engineering organisations if the goal of the community is to contribute feedback to the product and the nature of the product is to appeal to developers to use it better. However, if the goal of the community is to evangelise the platform, find more prospects and get users to interact with one another, then the community manager (CM) should sit in the SaaS marketing organisation than in the engineering or product organisations.

In terms of metrics to use to set the stage for your CM to deliver results, you can look at engagement metrics, which could manifest in the number of questions posted and answered on company-owned forums or third-party forums like Quora, Stack Overflow, G2 and others. When it comes to community membership, retention metrics can also be used to determine how many users want to be community members. The amount of time users spend on the knowledge centre or community forums can also be tracked and measured. The most popular and least popular documentation and content assets can be tracked. The number of actionable inputs received from the community can be used to evaluate the quality of community interactions and also for the betterment of the product.

Communities need a platform or a home to exist in. While SaaS brands can have a presence in third-party forums, they need to frequent the 'home ground' of a branded community platform. The CMs can be tasked with selecting the right platform based on the objectives of the community, something that will scale with growth in the number of users and the variety of use cases to support the metrics mentioned earlier. If the knowledge base that customer marketers and CSMs build can be offered to the community, then they can offer inputs to improve the content. The knowledge base should reside in the community platform and be available in a Wikipedia-like model where users can submit changes, additions and deletions.

One of the most important roles of the CM is to act as a bridge between the company and the community. Not everyone in the company is attuned to building and interacting with a community. There might be apprehensions because companies do fear customers interacting with each other—what if they share their frustrations and that leads to a domino effect? In the SaaS world, though, being open is a key characteristic. So, users can talk about the good, the bad and the ugly and learn. Letting users interact with one another requires quiet confidence from the company, and the CM plays a key role in opening up the company. Product managers, engineers, CSMs, the support team and the C-suite can be trained by the CMs to participate in the community and learn from their inputs and contributions.

The CMs need to define their roles. A CSM needs to know what to look for from the community and how to participate in it. Similarly, a PM will have a different objective and interaction pattern with the community. The CMs need to coach these personas on why they are being asked to participate in the first place and educate them on the vision and goals of the community and, more importantly, how their interactions can help further the cause. They need to see how their presence and actions help you achieve the vision and goals of the community.

Every community is a social organism and the rules of sociology apply here as well. Passive participants participate by being told to or may just log in to see what's going on. Information providers participate by answering questions posted by others, and sharing knowledge is their primary focus. Consultants participate by being asked questions or being tagged by others because they are known for their expertise. Opportunists participate for incentives like a quiz or a hackathon where there are prizes on offer. Functional participants focus on forming groups with like-minded individuals like people from the same country or vertical or persona. Self-motivated participants take the initiative and organise meetups on their own with users and seek to foster sharing of knowledge without much input from the SaaS brand. In these scenarios, the CM offers space or payment for food and beverages or gifts for the participants.

Smart CMs are good at identifying participant types, and they usually zone in on power users, who become the heroes of the story of the company and the platform. Power users need to be nurtured with care. A separate programme is warranted where they get access to more time, more documentation and more new features from your end. The reason for doing this is that power users also have the respect of the community. They are the alphas that others follow and are mini-influencers in their own right. Asking them to spend time every week answering questions, co-authoring content, participating in webinars and so on in return for swag, free access, visibility and publicity are good tactics from a CM point of view.

Power users can become an extended support team, which will take the pressure off your support organisation. In the SaaS world of empowered users, they like to find answers on their own as well. So they tend to ask other users or look up community forums to find them before they turn to your support organisation. Power users can also be trained to answer product and company questions, drive engagement and encourage more people to come forward with questions. They also need to be called out in the community as being special and power users so that others seek them out and also aspire to be them.

You can build content specifically for the community. Such content is typically crowdsourced and goes beyond just product content. Community content focuses on stories of users and how they succeeded, solved problems and overcame obstacles using your product. Getting users to share hands-on knowledge is a real benefit that you can offer to the company and the other users. You can also be clever in the way you use it. If you've come out with a new feature or capability, leveraging power users or early adapters to share their stories can potentially inspire the early majority to kick in!

Just like Quora has a vote-up feature that allows users to upvote answers to questions, a similar feature can add tremendous value to a community platform. For instance, if your PM wants to get feedback on a set of features, posting them on the community portal and asking for an upvote works well. Sometimes, open-ended questions can be seeded in terms of what users would like to see in the product one or two quarters down the line, and answers can be upvoted.

Community platforms that allow contests to be conducted work very well. Contests can be in the form of quizzes, hackathons and idea submissions. They can be fun and need not be all serious. Most SaaS companies whose products offer APIs for developers to build solutions conduct hackathons on specific themes to understand how creative users get when they use their platform.

Such events provide a lot of ideas to the SaaS marketer on the application of their technology and also serve as opportunities for getting power users and even enterprise customers as jury members.

A great community is necessary for a SaaS brand, not just for customer engagement and participation but also as a key part of the customer success model that frees up CSMs to focus on high-value conversations that have the maximum business impact.

An important factor is how the customer success team decides when to jump in to aid a customer and when not. Instead of leaving the decision to individuals, a framework should be put in place to help CSMs take these calls. The goal is balance. One key metric is the size of the account. Many SaaS companies assign shared CSMs for accounts of a certain size, and beyond that, they assign dedicated CSMs. This method is not scalable for accounts that are below a revenue threshold. However, even if you have assigned a CSM, if your customer does not take advantage of self-service, the knowledge base and the community, you might be missing a trick to save time, effort and cost for the customer and your company.

Self-service trumps dedicated customer success teams in certain scenarios, such as when a customer could benefit from another customer. Communities come in at this point, and despite the effort they take to set up and run, that effort pays off when users interact with one another to answer questions that your CSM might have had to. This technique works even if they do have a dedicated CSM! When customers have questions that fall into the FAQ bracket, no CSM should need to spend time on that. Linking users to the knowledge base and community when the account starts ensures that they go to these resources that are accessible, searchable and updated.

When the customer is in DIY (do-it-yourself) mode, even if they grow to a size where a CSM is warranted, as a SaaS marketer, you must not miss the cue and have them change their behaviour to DIFM (do-it-for-me) mode. With the knowledge base and community, they are provided with the resources they need to easily find their own answers. DIY users often attract other DIY users who will readily chime in with pointers and answers.

When your SaaS company is in a hyper-growth mode, it is akin to jumping off a cliff and building flight apparatus on the way down. Sometimes there just isn't enough bandwidth to be there for your customer at the moment they need you. This scenario can also happen depending on how international your SaaS brand is. Covering business hours in every time zone with your CSM team is hard, no matter how much you try. Internationalisation also brings to mind the availability of your knowledge base and your community support in different languages. Everything from the user community, feature requests, assets, recorded training and other resources need to be translated (preferably manually) into the core languages of operation to enable your customers to serve themselves, irrespective of the tier they are in.

Situations may arise where CSMs need to provide a personal touch. Onboarding is a critical phase, especially for larger accounts where there may be many users, sometimes numbering hundreds or thousands even. Here, there is no substitute for conducting onboarding events, building a personal connection with your new customer and understanding their business objectives, and how they are looking at value creation using your product. This personal time can also be used to orient users towards the knowledge base, the community and the self-service portal. They should feel that they are well supported across channels.

Some customers want the personal touch, no matter how digitally native they are. They still prefer to pick up the phone and call a CSM or hop on a virtual call to get the answers they need. As discussed earlier, this default behaviour needs to change, but don't rush it because that is a recipe for failure. Your traditional channels of outreach—email, phone, virtual meeting and chat—must all be covered, and a personal touch should be provided. However, you should keep referencing self-service, the knowledge base and the community while resolving their queries.

When customers are irate and disturbed, handling them with automated messages or just directing them to a knowledge base will not work. A personal response is needed unless it is a site-wide outage or a major downtime, in which case a communique that goes to all is called for. When that is not the case, however, then personal time is worth it. Irate customers can be detected on any channel. They may not necessarily be on a hotline with you. They could write you a strong email, tag you on social media or rage about you on a third-party review site. Listening across channels, understanding the context and responding are important.

If a customer is due to renew soon and/or has a lot of revenue at stake, you must first predict when that need for a personal intervention will come. By monitoring usage and tracking qualitative signals, CSMs can identify the health of an account based on several quantitative and qualitative factors and can identify when a customer shows a strong probability of churn. These triggers need human intervention, and CSMs and customer marketers need to work proactively and personally with the customers to resolve issues and turn the tide.

At the lower end of the pricing spectrum, there will be no one-to-one relationships. Even then, along with self-service, the knowledge base and the community, you need to provide at least one avenue for users to contact a live agent by phone, email or chat. Balancing and achieving a high level of performance both in self-service and service is crucial. While designing self-service, the factors that lead to service design—being empathetic, not letting the user feel abandoned and being timely in responses—must be considered.

Customer support teams never have to get involved. While this may be counter-intuitive, the customer success team plays a huge role in a strong self-service experience. The only difference is that it is intelligently automated and minimally staffed.

One of the most important contributions of self-service is feeding the enterprise funnel. The right time, the right trigger and the right usage can all be useful indicators to know when a sales representative or an SDR can call on the customer and offer them a plan to a higher tier where they have an account executive and a CSM dedicated to them.

Getting Users to Use: The SaaS Marketer's Role

Normally, getting users to use the service would be the responsibility of the customer success team exclusively, but the marketing team has a key role to play in the self-service scheme of things as well as in traditional enterprise engagement models. Just as marketing inspires prospects to try out your

SaaS brand, there is equal scope for marketing-led inspiration to get customers to use the service after purchasing it. Now one might ask why that is needed because they've evaluated the service and bought it. However, users are not necessarily convinced about procuring your SaaS service.

In certain scenarios, despite this being a user-driven purchase cycle, many users in the customer account may not be sure of the value of the service. When a control group of users has evaluated a product, there are scores of others for whom the service has been procured but who are not necessarily as keen or knowledgeable about it as the main users. Segmenting users is the first step that SaaS marketers need to take to get users to start using. If you look at the pre-purchase stage, there is scope there as well to get the trial users to see the full value of the service.

There are different types of pre-purchase users. Users who have logged in but not completed onboarding need to be nudged to finish. Users who have used the trial features and are at the end of their trial period need to be targeted to sign up. A successful trial with no conversion doesn't mean much. Contacting them at the midpoint and close to the end point of the trial can be effective. Users who use your product on a free plan but do not upgrade to the next level need to be targeted with feature restrictions to create a yearning to get the full power of the platform, for which they need to upgrade.

In a post-purchase scenario as well, there are many types of users, and each needs to be identified and dealt with uniquely. To create the segments, your SaaS platform needs to capture many different types of information:

1. Business metrics: User acquisition source, CLTV, monthly recurring revenue (MRR), retention rate, churn rate and free trial conversion

2. Usage metrics: User activation rate, user adoption rate, customer journey milestones, user onboarding stages
3. User demographics: Company name, size, revenue, job title, demographic data, industry, geography, size of the user team

SaaS marketers need to work closely with the product management and engineering teams to capture the factors of segmentation they need to dynamically create user segments and implement action plans to engage with each uniquely.

New users are the most obvious segment. They are those that may have signed up hours or minutes ago. This segment is also important to engage with because the first impressions and first few steps for a new user are indicative. If the product experience is confusing or its value and usage are not immediately apparent, users are likely to churn. As discussed in the previous section, new users need carefully planned onboarding and tracking to see if they move ahead in their journey.

The UX goal is to get them to a moment where they feel that they can use this platform and get value from it. Some companies use overlays to show new users what to click on and why. They see a journey laid out for them that tells them what to try first and what next. They can be sent tips to get started via email or WhatsApp (if they have opted in) or a native chatbot that works within the product. Sending checklists also works to let the users know how many steps they need to take to configure the product for themselves and start active usage.

There are users who have gone past the first phase but haven't used the features that you believe are the most important. Emails come in handy when they are not logged into the product, and in-app messages can be used while they use the product. These emails need not be very descriptive but need to have just the right information and CTA and nudges like 'Looks like you haven't tried this' to make the user feel that they have missed out on something important. Make sure the email is contextual in that it outlines the things that the user has used so that they know it's meant for them and that your company cares about their usage.

The other type of email to send is if someone hasn't used the product in a while. 'We miss you' is a phrase that is often used in emails to create an urge in respondents to consider what is being said. If the user is not acting on this email, then an effort needs to be made to gather feedback and understand the reason for the churn. Disengaged, churning users are inevitable in a SaaS business. The key is to have a strategy to identify and try and minimise churn while learning from those customers who churn out.

Although, as marketers, we want our ideal buyer personas to use only our product, the reality may be different. These personas have their own goals. For instance, you may target a campaign manager to use your product. In reality, some product marketing managers (PMMs) could be using your product because, in their company, they are in charge of running campaigns. Users with different backgrounds will have different goals. SaaS marketers need to work on creating targeted messaging within the product that is personalised to the user's persona.

For a campaign manager versus a PMM, different user onboarding flows and in-app experiences can be built that speak to the role's aims. Campaigns depend on company type—those selling desktop products will run campaigns different from companies that sell mobile apps. Users could be from different countries, so the product can also adapt to refer to the country by name in product communications and share benchmarks for data by country. User requirements might be different according to company size. Larger companies may need help onboarding larger teams. So, a customised interface that guides them through that process would be welcomed based on their goal.

However, for all this, enough information needs to be collected. As we have discussed earlier, information can be gathered during the lead generation phase itself through a chatbot or a lead form, but that is restricted to buyers and does not cover all users. One of the best ways to collect data about your users is to get to know them as and when they sign up. At that point in time, they are eager to experience the product, so they do not mind answering a few questions. The data points around role, industry, geography, goals and the like can be asked and quickly assimilated, which will help you create better in-app experiences for these users.

If your SaaS business model allows for a forever-free model, then you could have a sizeable chunk of users who never upgrade to a paid plan. Now that's convenient for the user but a cost for you to serve them. The goal of the SaaS marketer is to convert free users to paid customers. One way to do it is to make the free user segment, especially the heavy users, want the paid features of your product so that they can improve their value. One example is analytics, which is typically a paid service. The other way to do it is to limit their usage to a certain number of activities, such as a certain database upload limit or no downloads—anything that gently prevents the picture from being whole.

A combination of in-app nudges, greying of premium feature zones and targeted emails works to achieve conversion. If you find that multiple users in a company have signed up for the forever-free plan and are using it, you can try to approach their boss. You can reach out to a decision maker in that company to show the data of the number of employees using your product to pitch a corporate (premium paid) plan.

Once users start using the paid plan, many of them may choose the lowest paid plan and stick to it, which represents the next challenge for the SaaS marketer. The approach here is to upsell more features that take them into the premium plan. The key to upselling features to active users who are on low-end paid plans is to determine when exactly the customer needs them instead of saying 'Here's something cool that you haven't tried. Why don't you try it?' Disabling useful features but keeping them visible to the customer also works. When they click on the disabled feature, they are told what it can do for them, why it isn't currently enabled for them and what they need to do (read upgrade) to get it.

Even loyal users who have none of these constraints on them need to be targeted by SaaS marketers. With SaaS, the bar keeps rising for each user category. Loyal users need to be nurtured not just for more usage and revenue but also for becoming brand ambassadors and references for other customers. Their NPS is usually above eight. Beyond this, there are many other goals for them—speak at your customer conferences, address media together and many other value-adding partnerships. A high NPS rating (by definition) means that they are ready to promote you and probably do it already.

Churned users also need a strategy to get back to active usage. There are many reasons why a user can churn. Marketers always assume that the product stopped adding value to them or they stopped believing in it. There are several other reasons why users stop using—financial constraints, changing technology landscape, changed jobs or changed locations. Understanding 'why' is important and can be done via email through direct questions, which can sometimes get open and honest answers.

Building a close working relationship with product teams is a must for SaaS marketers. Everything that we discussed earlier is only possible if the product architecture team and the marketing team have a strong working partnership. Now that doesn't happen often but there are a lot of possibilities when it does. Marketers can look at opportunities in the product experience like the welcome screen for users when they sign up. The welcome screen is a great place to get to know your customer because they are eager to start and will answer some of your questions if you place them along the way. A pod (joint working group) with marketing and product teams in it makes it possible. Everything you learn from the process is golden—role, company size, location—and you can deliver a personalised onboarding and usage experience. Data from product usage also adds to your customer data platform to create more detailed customer segments and buyer personas. Now with this information, if you start tracking usage, you will learn a lot more about your users than you did before.

The other benefit of marketing and product collaboration is product analytics. Product analytics is a window into the mind and soul of the customer. Why and what to measure is a question that is often trumped by a need to fill analytics dashboards with widgets. Marketers can partner with product teams to tag features to measure how many users use primary and secondary features. Defining an activation point that all users must be led through via product prompts, emails or checklists is an important output of marketing and product combining. All along this journey, goals can be set up and measured to see where different segments of customers end up and whether there are common bottlenecks for everyone that need to be removed.

NPS ratings are part of most CSM objectives and key results (OKRs). However, marketers can help gather NPS data when the user is deep into the product experience. The data can be gathered when the journey takes shape and successes have been found. The NPS questions should be asked at the absolute right time when the user is on a high after having accomplished something with your product. Choosing the right timing builds on the gratification that the user is already feeling, and they feel motivated to provide (positive) feedback, something that a CSM can't achieve in a personal engagement because there's always going to be a lag.

Making a segment of one a reality is now possible because SaaS products have digital envelopes that gather enough data and create enough insight to deliver bespoke experiences to their customers from personalised onboarding to nudges to complete customer journeys, including upselling to core features that they haven't used. Whether you do this via in-app nudges or email, marketers need to be part of most of the important UX discussions, data discussions, feature discussions, roadmap discussions and CSM discussions in your SaaS company so that they can help create the right level of product engagement that delivers value and helps your firm capture value.

Covering the Top, Middle and Bottom of the Sales Account Pyramid

The sales account pyramid typically has three layers. The top layer has the most coveted high-value accounts. The middle layer has more companies, but the accounts are not as lucrative as those at the top. The bottom layer extends the logic to have the maximum number of companies and the lowest revenue per customer. The same is true for an existing account pyramid and a prospect pyramid. The goal is to make sure that, irrespective of where a customer enters the pyramid, they move up.

The SaaS marketer needs to have strategies in place for all three segments and also needs to map these strategies to the type of sales model that the company has in place. We have already explored the self-service model, which is a low-cost model that can bring in revenue with programmatic automated marketing. Users learn the value of the product, how to buy it and how to use it without consulting a salesperson or customer service representative. However, to drive revenue from self-service, the volume of sign-ups that marketing drives needs to be very high, and the marketer should plan for that.

SaaS companies also have a transactional sales model where they have a para-sales team and a deal desk that is focused on driving high volumes of sales transactions, sales support and rapid onboarding of customers. Hence, SaaS companies can focus on the middle and, largely, the bottom of the pyramid when they find that a pure self-service model is not going to work out. Some customers and regions need a low to moderate touch. SaaS marketing needs to create workflows working with sales operations, inside sales and deal desks to move leads through the funnel in a low-touch model. Marketing supports inside sales representatives with content automation that converts leads to MQLs. Inside sales convert and close low-value MQLs on their own and pass on high-touch, high-value deals to the sales team. Support is managed through self-service tools, educational content and chatbot automation. Customers will have access to CSMs as needed.

These models are no-touch or low-touch. In both of them, SaaS marketers need to visualise the prospect-to-customer journey and customer-to-user journey to provide a seamless experience across multiple touchpoints. Create customer journey maps, process workflows, email nurture sequence maps, content marketing plans and other elements to get all teams—marketing, sales (operations, deal desk), product, customer success and support—on the same page.

The enterprise sales motion is the upper crest of any sales model. This model focuses on 'calling high', as they say in sales, and developing a deeper engagement model with current and potential customers so that the value of the SaaS solution is explained in detail and demonstrated as stated earlier in the discussion on pilots and POCs. SaaS marketing here is more traditional and closer to the non-SaaS world, but triads and quads play a key role in devising account acquisition and monetisation strategies. Sales representatives focus on a narrow set of target prospects directly supported by triads or quads. SaaS marketing focuses on making select decision makers aware, building relationships and building sales tools such as ROI calculators and sales enablement content that can be used for specific purposes. The customer success team partners closely with the customer marketing team to create the right onboarding experience and drive usage through the year. For enterprise sales, particularly, the path to selling SaaS isn't typically linear. In the past, salespeople have been able to sway a single person to close the deal, but now they have to create a consensus among a group of decision makers with buying power.

ABM works on account maps targeting enterprise accounts. It uses tools to identify when visitors from those accounts explore the website and works out the best path to a conversation. Segmentation is the structure and strategy that supports how you deliver value to your customers. You segment your customers because, economically and financially, you have to treat your customers differently. We'd all like to give every customer the white glove treatment, but it's simply not financially prudent, and we all have to live within some financial constraints.

Segmentation applied to customer marketing is as important as when it is applied to marketing and sales pursuits. It is a key step in ensuring that your marketing work is impactful to the entire sales model. Segmentation is done more for your benefit than the customer's because every customer wants to be in only one segment—your number one segment.

Customers may not agree with the way you have segmented them, but they tend to accept it because it is driven by financial reality. An account that is a global major that bills you for a few thousand a month cannot expect you to dedicate triad and quad resources to them just because *they* are a global major. Working across a sales model means segmentation is also done to allocate *your* limited resources (and no matter how big your company is, resources are always limited) and determine whether a high-touch model, a low-touch model or a tech-touch model needs to be used.

Segmentation in customer marketing and success helps drive the customer engagement model, which influences team headcounts, resources and the forecast for retention percentages. The amount of time spent by a CSM in an account is a major influencer in its retention percentage.

Segmentation can be done in many ways, not dissimilar to how you would segment the market. Territory segmentation is the most common where the customer success and marketing teams segment accounts based on region, city or country. In some cases, segmentation does not necessarily depend on the size of customers in a region. Sometimes, the local language, culture and other dependencies force the segmentation. This type of segmentation is typically seen in Europe, Latin America and South East Asia. If your home country is India, say, and you want to expand customer success and marketing across regions, it's best to build local teams that work in a hub-and-spoke model with your central team. There is a tendency to staff more in the home country where the majority of costumes and sales teams are located, but that should not deter you from expanding teams in other geographies even before you hit critical mass there.

On the flip side, segmenting by country/region will often lead to well-served and underserved regions, and some will have more customers than others, making it harder to pivot if newer regions start showing more promise. The customer success and marketing teams can't straddle different languages and cultures, so make sure the analysis is thorough before taking up region-based segmentation.

Segmenting CSMs and customer marketers by industry is also common because each industry has its own dynamic and workflows. So, expecting one CSM to know it all might be challenging. Again, not spreading oneself too thin is advisable because there are fifteen to twenty industries and each will have at least four or five sub-industries. Identifying and staffing CSMs is crucial to scalability and maintenance. Domain experts with CSM experience are not easy to find and hire, because most of them are functional specialists, not domain specialists. Training a functional specialist on domain skills may be more cost-effective than looking for someone with both.

CSMs can also be assigned by product, but that is not a common practice because CSMs need to provide a unified face to a customer that subsumes all products. They can leverage a PMM or PM or solutions architect to fill in the gaps. You do not want to create product silos across your CSM organisation.

Parameters such as customer organisation size, employee size and membership in the Fortune 100 group are also used to assign CSMs to accounts and to support the sales motion. The best way would be to align with the sales pyramid where the top tier gets dedicated support, and the CSM is assigned the way sales representatives are assigned. Matching sales segmentation creates harmony in collaboration and alignment across the triad and the quad.

If you segment the customer base by the revenue they give you, then their actual size and stature are not accounted for. A large multinational company (MNC) may bill a small amount with you, and hence, they get segmented to a lower tier. Can this customer be added to the same segment as an SMB who bills an equivalent amount? The potential for revenue can be an additional variable to avoid this. One is a 100,000-member company with billions in revenue, and the other is a 50-member company with a few hundred thousand in revenue. The first one has more potential.

The balance is difficult because the customers who pay you more get more of your attention. The smaller-revenue customers, irrespective of their size and potential, will not make as much of a dent if they churn. It's a constant battle between the here and now and the future, but the allocation of CSMs to accounts and segments is based on revenue contribution. Some companies use a ratio of CSM to accounts so that each CSM manages a certain multiple of his or her cost to the company. If the product and business are more mature, then this ratio can increase even further. If product instrumentation and CSM technology can remove manual effort at your end, then this model is scalable. The true marker of customer success and customer marketing impact is not how much revenue the accounts they manage give the company but the reduction in churn (revenue and customer churn) they can achieve.

The cost of customer success management and customer marketing should never be explicitly borne by the customer. The cost should be included in the subscription. The service is an innate part of the SaaS model and need not be called out separately. Even if the economics of charging for a CSM is appealing, a SaaS company should focus on the value they and customer marketers bring. The only exception would be if it is a top-tier customer and the service is highly customised, which requires non-standard effort on the CSM's part to add value to the customer.

The segmentation and CSM allocation model you choose should be open to change. If your customer is in a hyper-growth mode, then the rate of change is the highest (months, not quarters). Not changing will hurt the business. Changing fast does not mean changing without consideration for cost. The CSMs are a core part of the relationship between your company and the customer. Ripping out CSMs and reallocating them hurts relationships and revenue. You need to work out what the change means for each customer. If the account has seen a CSM churn, the change may irritate it further. Allocating a CSM who has worked unsuccessfully with the account earlier will be counterproductive. Other things to consider include upcoming renewals and deep client relationships (friendships can form between CSMs and clients).

5

Renewals and Expansions: The Engine of a SaaS Business

Influencing Renewals

SaaS businesses are all about renewals. Renewals are the baseline metrics that any SaaS business is evaluated on. However, the investment in customer acquisition cannot be compared with that of renewals. We discussed how important it is to invest in customer success and customer marketing. Renewal is where the real growth lies.

Customer retention is the number of customers at the end of a period (usually a year) compared to the same number at the start of the period. A renewal is said to take place when the customer actively renews their contract. Retention is said to take place when a customer decides to remain with you but not necessarily with an active contract. Renewal is what a SaaS business strives for at the most fundamental level.

To drive renewals, SaaS marketing needs to focus at the beginning on a superb onboarding experience with a solid customer marketing programme, deliver a great product experience and strive to make the customer an advocate of the solution both internally and to their peer group. Helping customers deliver the value that they expect and also sampled during a pilot or POC is key to a successful renewal. Sometimes, however, value delivery for one year is sufficient, and the customer, while satisfied, might not want to renew or build your solution in-house. Driving renewals takes a multifunctional and multipronged approach, with the SaaS marketer at the core.

Should a salesperson be responsible for renewing a customer account? Should a farmer be responsible? The world of SaaS works differently. The customer success team plays a key role in driving renewals and setting the stage for expansion. The CSMs are separate from the sales team and own every step of the customer journey after the sale from onboarding to product adoption, renewal and expansion. Existing customers are much more likely to drive more revenue for you than new business. Usually, 70 to 80 per cent of a SaaS company's revenue is delivered by existing customers. SaaS marketers need to be good account-based marketers to make sure that the customer organisation is warmed up and convinced about a renewal.

Customers who renew more than once already talk about you to their peer group, leading to more referral business, which beats having to chase down that peer group on your own. Many companies feel the sales function can play the role of a CSM because 'after all it's managing the customer'. However, CSM is a very specialised skill, and unless you want to erode your customer base, it shouldn't be compromised. Like most things, customer success orientation starts at the top. If the leadership in your organisation doesn't know or believe in customer success and customer marketing, making a success out of customer success and marketing is an uphill battle. Most SaaS companies, until they hit a certain scale, are founder-driven. So it behoves the SaaS marketer to educate the leadership, for the sake of total customer management, on the importance of hiring and nurturing CSMs.

Be it a subscription mode or a consumption model, CX and value realisation are key. The renewal team, either led by the CSM or managed by a triad or quad, needs to have more access to customers than anyone else in the company. Establishing a client feedback system that is both qualitative and quantitative helps strengthen the case for successful renewals. Some SaaS companies pair a renewal account manager to help 'close' the renewal on the sales side. Others keep the same account manager both for acquisitions and renewals, and they look at churn as a key metric.

Churn is the number of customers that don't renew their contract after their period of engagement. The SaaS benchmark is to keep it less than 5 per cent or at a maximum of 10 per cent. The holy grail of the customer success function is negative churn—where the revenue from renewals (including upsells and expansion) is greater than the revenue lost due to non-renewals. Churn leads to loss of revenue and wasted CAC. The CSMs, the customer marketers and the sales team need to have a process in place to reduce churn and keep it in check.

Like everything in SaaS, renewals are all about timing and process. You can't call a customer a month before renewal and tell them to renew. They need to be educated on the value of their investment if they haven't realised it themselves. They need to know at least a quarter prior (for an annual contract) or a week or ten days prior (for a monthly subscription renewal) that renewal is due. Renewal preparation starts from onboarding.

Once the customer is signed up, the sales team introduces the customer to their CSM who coordinates with the renewal team. A couple of weeks after onboarding, the CSM reviews the customer's usage of the product and calls with a check-up. If usage is low, customer marketers plan campaigns to galvanise usage with content, email campaigns and so on. A couple of months down the line, the CSM plans a QBR with the customer and, before that, reviews the customer's usage of the product. The CSM then reaches out proactively. If usage is still low, then a larger-scale user engagement is planned, with account-based events to drive usage and improved stakeholder management planned by marketing.

At the halfway point, the CSM does a health check and projects if the account has a good probability of renewal. At this stage, if usage hasn't picked up, this account needs to go into the red. The CSM needs to have a discussion on value delivery with the customer. This would also be a good time to upsell new features or a larger plan if the usage has been good. Marketing can help with compelling content assets that show the value that other customers have derived by upgrading and using new features.

Between the halfway point and a quarter before renewal, the CSM works on solidifying the expansion plan for the account or at least getting the renewal forecast to 100 per cent. A month or two before the renewal, the CSM initiates the business process at the account to ensure that the renewal paperwork happens on time and there are no procedural issues that can derail or delay it. There isn't much that marketing can do at this stage. A fortnight before the renewal, ideally, the process should close. Usually, especially in India, the process is always stacked towards the end of a quarter or year. Additional help from the company's leadership team should be taken at this stage to push things through at the client's end.

The involvement of the sales team in renewals should ideally be as a support function, much like the marketing function. The ownership should ideally be with the CSM. One of the main reasons for this is that sales teams often stretch themselves out working with many accounts. They are driven only by revenue and targets, which is fine because that's how you want them to be. They may look at renewals as a 'done deal' and not give them the attention and rigour that they need. The skill sets to retain accounts are different from those to acquire. Bring the sales team and their persuasive skills during important discussions.

Customer success teams use their own toolset, with tools such as Gainsight, to manage the renewal process. The reason is that CRM systems took some time to adapt their platforms to track renewals. The stages of the customer success process were not readily available in most CRM systems. Salesforce, for instance, now provides a customer success module and a marketing module along with their traditional sales. The renewal stages, dates and values need to be integrated into the sales view to give a single view of the customer to the company right from the time they enter the system as prospects to the time they convert as customers and start billing, renewing and expanding. Also, the part of the revenue that is renewable should be pointed out—the licence fee is but set-up charges are not. Like deals have a date of closure and probability of closure with a deal value, renewals also need to have a date and a probability of renewal.

Measuring the rate of churn is essential. Now a staple measure in all SaaS companies (we cover this in Chapter 6), the rate of churn should be discussed during reviews at all levels. The other aspect is rewards. Again, a practice that companies follow is to reward the sales team for acquiring new customers and meeting and beating targets. Teams that own the renewal goals should also be able to earn more than their salary by meeting and beating the renewal targets. Some companies fix a variable component for CSMs based on the overall renewal attainment for the company, which may not incentivise every CSM to be motivated to beat their individual number. Making the renewal number an individual target as well as a team target helps to drive the right type of renewal behaviour even among CSMs.

Renewals are dependent both on the human touch and the technology stack. Instrumenting the product to integrate with the CSM management tool to provide inputs to the CSM dashboard is essential for CSMs to be able to manage renewals at scale. Customer renewal ratings should be automatically computed qualitatively and published so that it is ready for CSMs to review. Over and above that, CSMs can add their qualitative input to make renewal ratings more holistic. If a customer has visited the cancellation page on the product, then an alert should go to the CSM immediately to take action. This type of design is also a key aspect of PLG.

For smaller customer segments such as the mid-market segment, CSMs are shared across tens of accounts and will have to rely more on aspects like self-service, documentation, the knowledge base and the community to help them retain and grow customer revenue. This aspect has been discussed in the previous chapters as to how a combination of marketing and product can help onboard, retain and renew customers.

There are cases where you need to let customers go. If they renegotiate their subscription with you to reduce the average unit price, are unreasonable and do not respect the features and benefits you provide them, an executive decision needs to be taken to let the renewal fall through.

This situation is rare, but when the time comes, the decision needs to be made for the greater good.

Renewals That Expand

There's nothing like inspiring existing customers to upgrade or expand their scope of engagement with a SaaS business. As discussed in the first chapter, expansion can be in terms of the number of users or features or volume, depending on the type of SaaS business model your company runs. SaaS businesses need to increase the value of customers over their lifetime because generating more revenue from new customers is more expensive than increasing revenue from existing customers. The pandemic has made selling and acquiring new customers more difficult due to the lack of physical interactions and businesses becoming more cautious.

To achieve this, SaaS businesses need to invest more in customer success. If the CSM does a good job in ensuring renewals, there is already a baseline in place to talk about expansions as we saw in the previous section. Generating additional revenue from an installed base is 70 per cent cheaper than doing the same from a new customer. Saving costs while increasing revenue is a key the CEO and chief financial officer (CFO) consider imperative, especially given the number of SaaS businesses receiving high levels of funding with little or no profits to show for it.

Focusing on expansion and increasing the coveted CLTV/CAC ratio is the bedrock of SaaS business performance measurement. This measure explains how efficiently the SaaS business earns back what it spent on acquiring a customer and how it maximises the revenue that is being earned from that customer. When customers expand their subscriptions or purchase additional features and services from the SaaS company, their renewal base increases. Therefore, they contribute more revenue each time they renew, which means that it takes less time for SaaS vendors to realise their CAC. Investors love shorter earn-back periods, and, more importantly, it makes good business sense.

SaaS marketers can work in multiple ways with CSMs and sales teams to drive expansions. Upsells are the most common form of customer expansion and involve selling a more expensive plan or adding additional features that are priced separately like advanced analytics. The basis for upgrades in plans depends on the type of SaaS business. Broadly, upgrades could be based on capacity or volume or number of users or depth of analytics required. Upselling usually works when the customer has bought into the value of the base product. Their willingness to buy increases dramatically once they find the baseline works well for them.

Growth is about value discovery and realisation, not bombarding customers with nudges to upgrade or keep buying more. Let them soak into the experience and realise the outcomes. Then you can talk about upselling. Companies that offer the freemium model or the forever-free model bet on the quality of their product to do the heavy lifting for them because, as we discussed earlier, they cannot afford to support droves of free customers. Here, a capability upgrade that the customer does on their own is considered an expansion via upselling.

Cross-selling occurs when complementary products or related products are added to the subscription package. For instance, if you use a CRM to manage the sales management process, adding the marketing module or the customer success module to it is a cross-sell. Cross-sell is a more involved process than an upsell because the customer needs to perceive your capability as being equally strong in the module being cross-sold versus what they are using currently. Marketing has to play an important role in ensuring that the SaaS brand is associated with all the product categories that the company offers and not just with the primary or strongest one.

In the CRM example, Salesforce, say, is a well-known software for sales management, and they cross-sell marketing and customer success modules. However, other tools like Marketo and Gainsight are more popular for marketing automation and CSM respectively. Similarly, HubSpot, which might be popular for inbound marketing and automation, may not be the most popular name in the business when they try to cross-sell their CRM. In this era of open architectures and integration, customers can buy best-in-class products and integrate all of them.

The more products you can sell to a single customer, the less likely they are to churn because they are more invested. The more integrated a customer is with a business system, the harder it is for them to switch. According to the SaaSRadar report by Gainsight and McKinsey & Company, mature SaaS companies (US$25 million to US$75 million in revenue) that cross-sold multiple products to one-third of their customer base had the least churn.[4] Product stickiness helps to secure renewals, reduce churn and increase CLTV.

Bundling is a common expansion strategy that combines elements of both upselling and cross-selling. A bundle offers complementary products to provide customers with a wider range of solutions for a total cost that is lower than the sum of the individual costs. For instance, the Adobe Creative Studio bundle includes all their tools at a price that is lower than if you bought each of them separately.

Along with additional products, more advanced analytics and reporting can be combined.

Since the expansion process is closely tied to and depends upon renewals, the same structure can be followed for expansions as for renewals. However, SaaS companies use different models. Usually, the sales team is tasked with adding 40 per cent over the first year's annual contract value (ACV) in the second year. Sales teams usually carry expansion targets, and CSMs carry renewal targets. However, if the triad and the quad work like they are supposed to, this should not make a difference. Expansion also occurs when unserved parts of an account start using the same product that you sold to one division or team. Marketing can play a huge role in expanding an account's SOI to drive more expansion. We will explore that in the next section.

Knowing when to nudge an account to expand is also critical. Product analytics can provide good guidance on this issue to CSMs, sales representatives and marketing teams. Data-driven timing is always a good indicator to start talking about expansion. Start with a programmatic nudge, either through in-app notifications or an email-based nurture. After that, if the customer picks up the hint, the conversation flows easier with the sales and customer success teams but not always.

If your avenues of expansion are only adding more seats (licences), your options are limited despite the CSM's best efforts. The reason is that customers are very good at managing and optimising what they have bought from you. In many cases, MRR doesn't increase despite the customer being happy. So, using only additional features and additional seats as drivers of expansion may limit you. Instead, the product should be modularised to such an extent that there is a natural requirement for customers to use advancements as they progress on their journey. If they use your platform to run a campaign, for instance, their baseline audience size can be 1,000 contacts, but if they want to do more, they need to buy more credits. If you give them a larger contact quota at the base package level, then you lose that as a lever of expansion.

Create stages in everything that the customer uses because as they climb those stages, they will expand their scope of work with you. Again, the stages should not constrain a customer, and they should not think that there is greed involved. The UX should flow seamlessly. So, if a client uses your platform to run campaigns, pricing should be according to database, clicks, conversion rates and automation nurtures so that you create more avenues for expansion rather than just rely on seats and features. These additional avenues make strong cases for expansion, and the conversations with the CSMs and sales reps become shorter.

Expansion needs to have a more holistic approach compared to renewals because CSMs are not in charge of product plans, sales plans or even pricing. Triads and quads need to work together along with the product to make the process of driving expansions efficient and scalable.

SOI and How to Build It

Acquiring new customers comes with significant cost and effort by the sales team. To retain and grow customers, we have seen how CSMs and customer marketers can add value, but the sales team must also not drop the ball. Sales teams tend to give a lot of attention to customers while they are in the pipeline and about to close, but once that is done, the proverbial ball tends to be dropped.

The other risky aspect of managing account relationships is relying on a relationship with a single individual who works in that account. If this person were to leave or get moved to a different team, the account and revenue could be put in jeopardy. Evaluating how deep the relationship with an account is, especially your top 100 accounts, is important. Measuring the SOI is critical to this evaluation.

An SOI can be expanded in many ways. If a customer asks for information or a report that may take time, ask if a presentation can be made to them and their peers or manager who will consume the report. Often, customers will not expose vendors very high in the organisation, but this could be a way to try.

If access to a higher level does not work, then ask for a meeting with the customer's peer group, which might be less intrusive for them. Improving your SOI strengthens your account position and makes it harder for competitors to replicate. They may find it easier to do so if it is just one person that you know that they need to sway. Having higher-level contacts and contacts across functions makes upselling and cross-selling less constrained instead of just getting a yes or no from your primary contact.

Once you have acquired a customer, acquiring an additional set of contacts is not difficult. Acquiring an additional set of customers is harder! Your SOI allows you to leverage the contribution of the contacts close to your primary decision maker, helps you have more friends in the account and aids you to sell your product to different parts of the company. There are always obvious players in a buying centre—decision maker, approver or influencer—who you would have mapped during the sales process.

However, you need to go beyond the obvious if you want to build a real SOI—your decision maker's peer group, the sceptics who were opposed to your deal, the decision makers' subordinates who did the actual evaluation or the payables coordinator who pays your invoices! These are useful contacts. So, how do you go about building an SOI? As a SaaS marketer, you can work with your triad or quad to use many tools to identify who to target. The SOI is not random and needs a carefully conceived approach to building relevant connections within an account.

Organisation charts are the right place to start understanding the lay of the land. For much larger accounts, narrow it down to the region or business unit you are selling into. If the chart is not readily available, use LinkedIn or DiscoverOrg or ZoomInfo (acquired by DiscoverOrg) to help you create a map and set of targets. The static chart itself doesn't tell you the whole story. Initially, who can be part of the influence fabric is unknown. Titles don't provide much information. Using the organisation chart and mapping your primary contact there, you can work up, down and sideways until you find out who influences who. The reality is that most people you engage with as prospects or even customers don't make the final call. They all play a specific role. The organisation chart gives you a crude map to start.

Some event companies have a strange approach that, even more strangely, works. They send information about a particular event to about twenty of the top executives in your company. Now, as a marketer, you may ignore it as another cold email from an event company, but it has novelty for a CFO or a CIO who doesn't get these types of emails. They may forward it to you to get your attention. Now, this approach is spamming and not something that you should follow, but it gives you an example of how having multiple entry points for prospecting can trigger an SOI into action.

If the event company had just bombarded the marketing manager with the same email, it would have ended in spam.

Prospects can go cold even while they are discussing a deal with you. So, use the organisation chart to keep others informed that you are speaking with your primary contact and would love to brief them on the goings-on. If you identify multiple customer employees and keep them informed of the conversation, keeping it going even if the primary contact loses interest becomes easier. Your company and brand can also be part of water cooler conversations because the right people in your SOI are getting your nudges.

Using the organisation chart, sometimes targeting individual contributors helps to create a groundswell that can 'take you to the boss' who might have gone cold or is not responding to your email outreach, campaigns or even sales conversations. Getting a recommendation from a team member who says 'Maybe you should check them out' or 'They have been trying to reach you for a few days and haven't heard back' can go a long way in getting them to respond. Sending a copy of the email by using the organisation chart and determining SOI is also a good tactic. The recipient might not respond but others cc'd may if you have done your homework.

In the SaaS world, the most important buyers are the users. Using the techniques described earlier to target individual contributors who are users can also create a groundswell that will either lead to a conversation with a buyer or, if it is an existing account, lead to a conversation with a new set of users within the same account.

While navigating the organisation charts and building your SOI, you must note that different members of the SOI have different goals, pain points and OKRs. If your SaaS company provides a campaign management platform, that product aligns directly with the growth marketing manager's OKRs (meet lead targets), but it needs to speak differently to the CMO's OKRs (drive new revenue), CFO's OKRs (reduce CAC) and CSM head's OKRs (reduce churn, increase CLTV) and, hence, needs to be positioned differently.

In larger companies, sometimes procurement is centralised, and sometimes it is not. Even within a country, there may be differences. Here, SOI comes in real handy because a buyer in one business unit can be a referrer for you in another business unit. Central procurement will not be involved here nor will they question why two different business units are working with the same vendor. If they do, then they may ask for a central contract with you, which is also not bad.

For your campaign management platform, there may be different types of marketing teams in the same company to reach out to individually, and they may not talk to each other. In larger companies or in hyper-growth companies where the level of decentralisation is very high, such a situation is possible. The organisation chart can be used to pitch the same solution to different marketing teams to use the SOI to your advantage.

Sometimes, not receiving a response doesn't mean they haven't read it. Of course, there's no way for you to know without the help of technology. Tools like Demandbase and ZoomInfo give you a lot of account-based insight on which accounts actually visit your website, and correlating your outreach with activity on your web properties can give you a good sense of what happens behind the scenes. If the follow-ups are effective, then there is a good chance that a demonstration will be scheduled shortly with the account.

How to Plan for Renewals

We touched upon the renewal process briefly and what it takes to get it right. SaaS companies are beginning to take renewals more seriously than before and not as a foregone conclusion. Increasing customer retention can positively impact profitability because it reduces the S&M component of the operating spend. SaaS companies meeting their annual number with 70 to 80 per cent coming from existing accounts and the rest from new accounts is not uncommon. Renewals drive CLTV, a part of which earns back the CAC incurred as quickly as possible. They also drive up profits and long-term growth.

Planning for renewals starts right at the beginning with customer onboarding. Poor onboarding can scar customers for the remainder of your contract, and it's an uphill battle from there. First impressions count a lot here because investments have been made, buy-ins have been taken, everyone involved is watching the progress of the project, decision makers need to look good for having taken the decision, and users need to get their hands on the product and see the value. In short, there's a lot at stake. Just 'executing' a successful onboarding and 'ticking all the boxes' to say we have done it is not enough. The ideal result from onboarding should be that the user can adapt your solution to their advantage.

Communicating throughout the contract period with the users and the SOI is important to drive renewal success. Irrespective of whether usage is flagging or going up, being proactive with the customer is important. Active listening during client meetings helps to collect the right kind of feedback that is actionable. Combining data from the product with qualitative insights from the triad and the quad, sharing that with the customer and getting their feedback is a vital output of proactive communication.

Preparation for a renewal starts from the beginning of the contract term. We discussed the process in detail at the start of the section. Understanding customer workflows and user journeys early on helps to address challenges and deliver value. Creating a positive product experience that is personalised to their goals is key. Focus on creating value, and the revenue will follow. Communication with users, decision makers and the SOI should be consistent and clear from the start. Mark clear moments in the twelve-month cycle that make the biggest impact on renewal success—onboarding, 30-day mark, 90-day mark, 180-day mark, 270-day mark and finally the 330-day mark or the last month. At each point, assess the health of the account and work with the triad and the quad on mitigating risks if any.

Expansions sometimes take place during the contract period itself and do not wait for renewal. On other occasions, expansions that take place along with the renewal are tagged as 'renew and expand'. This kind of expansion is often desirable because it keeps the revised cycle in line with the start of the contract. If expansions occur mid-year, then the expansion component has its own renewal cycle and the original ACV has its own renewal cycle. At some point, both need to be combined and brought to the same time.

Some SaaS companies have escalation desks for the highest tier of accounts. So, beyond the CSM, the triad and the quad, there is a group that can provide valuable assistance at a short notice. This team is mainly reactive and not a support team. It is a high-level customer care team that comes together for the company's most valuable accounts.

Having playbooks that can be repeatable across different accounts is key to ensuring that the renewal process is not people-dependent but process-dependent. The process should document the twelve-month life cycle, key milestones, work to be done by the triad and the quad before the key milestones, data from the product and usage statistics to monitor, how to handle customer escalations, low usage scenarios, how to secure the renewal in advance and so on. Develop renewal playbooks based on those processes so that all teams are informed of their roles and can contribute to improving the process.

We have discussed the roles that CSMs, customer marketers and sales representatives play in the renewal cycle. Care should be taken to not overwhelm the CSM with a ton of product capability and technical complexity. As the number of customers increases and the product or platform evolves, the creation of specialist roles that can combine to work on renewals and expansion is essential.

The CSMs can be focused on long-term goals that go beyond the year such as driving adoption, delivering value and realising great CLTV. They focus on hitting the twelve-month renewal planning milestones, planning and attending QBRs and customer training and feature adoption. At the nine-month mark, the renewal manager (RM) can start the renewal conversation, working closely with the CSM. Retention is the sole objective of an RM.

The RMs initiate the renewal conversation with the customer and ensure that the renewal agreement is aligned to customer goals and that any hurdles such as satisfaction issues, low usage, low ROI and the like are resolved by working with the triad or the quad. In some companies, RMs report to the CSMs, and in others, they are part of the sales team. Hiring RMs is not easy as it is still not a standard role. More experienced sales representatives might not covet the role, nor would CSMs. This role would probably be good for someone who is in the inside sales function to start their sales career because RMs need to be driven by numbers. They must also have good relationship-building skills, be able to create and run processes, solve problems and, of course, be customer-centric.

In other SaaS companies, farmers or expansion sales managers focus on growing accounts by finding new opportunities to sell more features, add more seats and upgrade the product usage capacity. They expand the SOI in the customer account and use all of the expansion levers discussed in the previous section to increase CLTV from the existing accounts. Farmers are part of the sales organisation. Such roles proliferate in larger SaaS companies, and stakeholders need to collaborate and communicate in one voice with the customer. No team member should reach out to the customer out of turn, and there should be alignment on who speaks to the customer and when. The customer must be aware of the proper communication channels.

Apart from alignment on communication, there needs to be alignment on metrics so that they all amount to the same thing—drive usage and engagement metrics to drive renewals, which, in turn, help expansions and increase CLTV overall. Larger accounts can have individual targets, and mid-market accounts can have group targets so that fluctuations in the fortunes of a few accounts don't derail the overall renewal and expansion process or goals. We discussed how the renewal process should begin once onboarding has been completed for new customers and for existing customers once the renewal opportunity has closed for a year. Beginning early helps plan early. The renewal team needs to communicate with the customer when four or five key milestones have been reached.

Prior to that, the team needs to evaluate the indicators that the customer gives directly via feedback or indirectly via their usage or lack of it of the product. The feedback should be taken as an opportunity to communicate with them about adoption, renewal or expansion. A good practice is to encourage early renewals to take the edge off the pressures of the last week of the quarter and the last quarter of the year. They also save time and effort. Sometimes, they help to shore up revenues when some of the middle quarters of the year do not go too well. Customers can sometimes opt for early renewals because they want to avoid the waiting line at the finance desk or the internal process they need to follow to make the deal happen. Early renewals can be encouraged by offering discounts, expanding users and sealing the pricing for multiple years.

When it comes to the SMB segment or the paying but low MRR segment, it is best to renew their accounts automatically and programmatically. Many of them may be paying through credit cards, so charges can be scheduled with prior intimation. Contracts can be made auto-renewable, and via the self-service portals, renewals can be administered.

In all these cases, renewals need to be accurately forecasted so that the sales and finance teams can add them to their business forecasts for the shareholders and the board. Factors such as usage, NPS, account health indicators and customer sentiment contribute towards renewal forecasts, which the RM needs to consider in the forecast update with the renewal probability expressed as a percentage. When combined, all these inputs present a clearer picture of customer health. Focusing on forecast accuracy is essential because a SaaS business is about continuum and existing accounts account for a bulk of the revenue. Forecasting helps to assuage business owners and shareholders. Accuracy needs to be celebrated.

6

Building a SaaS Marketing Team

Different Types of SaaS Marketing Structures

SaaS companies, like others, come in different shapes and sizes. One advantage of this segment, given its relative age as compared to other segments, is that most SaaS companies have not grown into global behemoths requiring n-dimensional matrices to manage them. Since the business is built on collaboration, the SaaS organisational structures are also simpler, while having their own distinct identity.

The first question to ask is—where does SaaS marketing sit in an organisation structure? Marketing's position is driven almost directly by how SaaS founders and founding teams view marketing. We will cover that in detail in a later section. The SaaS marketing team typically has its own seat at the C-level executive table or reports to the chief growth officer—a role that many SaaS companies have that combines S&M efforts.

SaaS marketing leadership structures are also driven by where the dominant market for the company is versus where the company's home market is. Typically, India-headquartered SaaS companies tend to keep their SaaS marketing leadership in-country. If they expand into North America or Europe or other markets, they may move their top leadership there and hire a CMO in the dominant market and have VP and ranks below VP located in India to provide scale and cost benefits to the company.

Also, in terms of the marketing organisation, SaaS companies use different structures. Typically, there are centralised and decentralised parts of the marketing organisation. Ideally, SaaS companies need a centralised structure in the initial phase of the company's growth, because the marketing team is also, along with the sales and the customer success teams, finding its feet. Triads and quads are formed and start to engage with customers. In a centralised structure, the SaaS marketer can drive brand, demand generation, product, content and DevRel programmes consistently while integrating with other functions in the SaaS organisation like sales, customer success, product, engineering and others.

However, given the nimble and 'start-uppy' nature of SaaS companies, they tend to also have decentralised structures, where marketing is not a specialist role that anyone plays but is something that everyone does. Over time, despite hiring marketing specialists, such companies do not go for a centralised approach. They leave marketing decentralised to keep things nimble, letting the central marketing organisation focus more on corporate functions like media relations, brand and website. Areas like demand generation, product marketing and others sit within the business units or product teams or regional teams.

The larger, more stable SaaS organisations achieve a middle ground by having a central marketing hub that is usually located in the country where the majority of the workforce resides (usually a country like India) and regional marketing teams that cover the field and local public relations (PR), while digital marketing is driven centrally. Marketing leadership sits where global leadership sits.

Core Parts of a SaaS Marketing Organisation

Corporate Marketing

This section covers media relations, analyst relations (AR), content, SEO, social media and design. Websites rarely reside within corporate marketing because, in SaaS companies, the website is the product, as we have seen in earlier sections. Corporate events teams handle internal summits and roadshows and large global events that represent the brand on a global stage.

Growth

Growth is a new term for demand generation. This function has the field marketing team, the digital marketing team and the all-important marketing operations team that owns the martech stack and also runs the MOFU nurture sequences. Field marketing, depending on the structure of the marketing organisation, reports to either the central marketing team or is distributed across regional marketing teams.

Product and Partner Marketing

Product and partner marketing covers the go-to-market part for core parts of the SaaS products, features and platform and partners closely with the growth (PMMs carry OKRs to bring in new users for the product and participate in lead generation, field events and review ad copy and nurture sequences), the content (they also drive thought leadership for their products) and, of course, the product and engineering teams. Partner marketing is also an under-represented aspect of SaaS marketing. Technology partners, independent software vendors (ISVs), resellers, regional partners and SaaS companies are a part of marketplaces, and there's a lot that needs to be done to promote your product through partners.

DevRel

Usually, DevRel does not sit in marketing but should, given the open nature of SaaS architectures. DevRel is key to community building, which is key to making self-service work and taking the pressure off the customer success and support teams, especially when the number of customers scales up. Even if the reporting is not a straight line to the SaaS CMO, efforts must be made to create at least a dotted line reporting to keep community engagement consistent, even when activities are dispersed.

Brand Identity

One of the biggest risks of a dispersed marketing organisation is the dilution of brand identity. Invariably, someone in some corner of the world does not follow the brand book and uses the logo in a wrong manner or a colour palette or font in an inadvisable manner. Detecting and reversing this becomes a nightmare for a creative head or a brand manager.

Brand Positioning and Messaging

Every SaaS brand has a messaging house, which has the key messages that convey the crux of the vision and mission of the brand, the reason to exist, the brand promise and value statements about the benefits that the brand provides customers. If these do not come out consistently in every booth, every video, every presentation, every advertisement and every email, then the brand comes across as being disjointed.

Product Positioning and Messaging

Product positioning and messaging is a crucial part of the messaging house and comes across in the way the product is pitched and described in field and digital campaigns, websites, social media and other places. If product positioning and messaging is not consistent, then it can confuse your audience of buyer personas.

Lead Management and Data Visibility

One of the biggest challenges SaaS marketers face in ROI calculations is the availability of consistent data that flows across marketing automation, CRM and product usage and billing systems. The more dispersed the marketing function, the bigger the challenge in consistently maintaining data across the life cycle of a customer.

Budgeting and Spending

Who owns the budget? That's a key question when estimating marketing budgets. In a dispersed organisation, how does marketing spend get calculated and reconciled to ensure that the spending is to an integrated plan and does not exceed what is truly needed?

The interplay between all these teams is the secret sauce of what makes SaaS marketing work.

Corporate Marketing

Corporate Communications

Corporate communication is one of the oldest functions in marketing, as old as the media! However, it is a channel that is often not understood by SaaS founders and marketers. Those who are 'media savvy' leverage it to the hilt, but those who are not so savvy view it with scepticism, almost like black art, and relegate this function to sending out a few press releases on wire services, providing a few authored articles and giving a few interviews. As a result, SaaS companies do not know how to get the best out of either their in-house corporate communications professionals or the media agencies they work with.

The key to making your PR programme successful is to run it like a demand generation function. Like in demand generation, your channels are set, but how you use them, who you target and what the message is determines what gets you the best return. Similarly, in PR, your corporate communications employee or media agency has access to the same set of journalists that other companies do. Journalists are not segmented as precisely as markets are. One person may cover technology, start-ups, business and finance. Maybe you can have a few who have industry expertise in sectors such as telecom or retail.

If you leverage your messaging house, create themes that you want to take to the media (corporate themes, product themes and regional themes) and build a media universe that matches those themes, right down to the individual journalist. That then sets the platform for a meaningful media relationship to begin. The word 'relationship' is important because news coverage tends to be all about 'newsy' elements like fundraisers, announcements and launches. Your PR agency will always tell you that they need something newsworthy. Here, the skill of making something newsworthy comes in.

Here are a few tips that SaaS marketers can use to create more newsworthy items:

1. Focus on what's between announcements: Getting quoted when you have something to announce is easy, but the real test is how you stay in the news in between announcements.
2. Link your product to a megatrend: If your product helps collect dues more efficiently, then link it to

collections issues that plague economies and present it in that manner to the media. Hire an economist and conduct a study on how receivables and dues form a significant part of a nation's gross domestic product (GDP) and use that as a hook.

3. Build on other announcements: If your trend has been spoken about by a competitor or an industry leader and that has been in the news, use that as a reference to give to the journalist.
4. Work on media planning thematically: Use three or four themes in your messaging house with an outreach plan for each and run them like a swim lane.
5. Meet the media to educate even when there is no story: This is a great way to sow the seeds for later coverage. Conduct a training session on a new trend or technology with no expectation of coverage. If your product can be experienced via a demonstration, send them demonstrations the way you would a prospect.

AR

The function of AR secures third-party validation for your technology and your market position. Analysts work independently as subject matter experts or as part of research firms. They need to be engaged with and briefed on your product and market movements. They always seek to learn more about different vendors. The best analysts have an ear for both vendors and buyers. So they are able to provide sage advice to both.

Depending on which industry your SaaS business focuses on, the analyst groups may change. Gartner, International Data Corporation (IDC) and Forrester are the big three that cover most enterprise technology segments, especially cloud-based and SaaS segments. Forrester has, over the years, focused more on the CMO persona, whereas IDC and Gartner remain focused on the CIO persona from the buyer side.

Many SaaS companies do not understand the function of AR well. They feel that customer validation is more important than analyst validation, but analyst validation provides credibility that customers value when they need to decide which vendors to invite to the table for a request for information (RFI) or when investors need to decide whether they should invest in your company or not.

However, AR, unlike PR, has a longer gestation time. Analysts start with not knowing your company, or they may have heard of you in passing. They may have a neutral, positive or negative view of your capabilities and, as an extension, your place in the consideration set for a vendor grouping (Gartner calls it magic quadrant, while IDC calls it market scape). A place in this vendor grouping and your relative position with respect to others is what you are vying for.

The AR function needs an internal champion, an AR manager who coordinates briefings with the analyst universe, and a product champion who works with the AR manager on the right kind of messaging to be given to each analyst based on their areas of coverage and prior publication history. The spokesperson in the initial interactions can be an executive, but as the relationship matures, product marketers and PMs can also take analyst calls.

While the top-tier analysts are coveted, they are also expensive and usually charge an annual fee for unlimited access to their analysts and their research. If your SaaS company cannot afford it, you can go for unpaid briefings, and if your product story is strong, you do stand a good chance of coverage. Cultivating relationships with boutique analyst firms that may not be as big as the big three is also important, but you should have a niche following that your buyer persona and the investor community follows. You can also buffer your internal AR team with an external agency that can help build relationships with analysts in the initial years, and then, you can take over and handle it independently.

SEO

We discussed the importance of content and discoverability in the earlier chapter. Having a strong SEO engine to drive organic traffic to your SaaS website is critical for several reasons. Over time, your organic traffic should be 70 per cent of your web traffic as compared to paid. Your business then attracts its buyer persona without you having to spend as much to acquire them. So, SEO reduces CAC, provided you craft the right kind of freemium/trial model and a product UX that can move users from free to paid.

SEO is almost a science now that search is more than twenty years old. Every year, Google updates its algorithms and increases the emphasis on writing quality content as being the key to driving rankings up. Google reduces the need for black hat SEO techniques like keyword stuffing, fake linking and other tactics companies use to get their website up on the publishing scale. Instead, Google asks you to follow simple rules like appropriate title tags, meta description, updated content, right keyword density (1.5 to 2 per cent), right URL structure, quality backlinks and interlinked content. You will hit most of these requirements if you focus on the user, readability and navigability. There are no shortcuts in the world of SEO. Good quality content that keeps the user in mind ensures that you will do well.

Depending on the size of your company, you may not be able to staff a full-time SEO specialist and may need to hire an agency. While an agency is acceptable to get you started with the basics of SEO, moving this role in-house is recommended. The specialist then works to understand the buyer persona, product and content roadmap and then crafts an SEO strategy that will get you the best ranking results that no agency can match.

The SEO specialist should have a strong working relationship with the content team or, ideally, be a part of the content or inbound marketing team. Some companies have a larger SEO team that divides on-page and off-page SEO between themselves.

Content

The content factory is a key team that a SaaS marketer builds to power the discovery of the brand via SEO and through other channels like social media. Think of the content factory as a publisher would—you have an editorial team, writers, designers and marketers. Think of yourself as running a media company that produces valuable content for your buyer persona.

Content teams usually follow the structure of editorial teams:

1. Content editors keep the writing tight and in line with the voice of the brand as enshrined in the brand book.
2. Content strategists focus on what to write, with inputs from the executive team, product teams and SEO teams.
3. Content publishers focus on how to promote the content on various owned, earned and paid media.

4. Content writers write short-form and long-form content (the skill sets are different).
5. Copywriters write very short-form copy for advertisements.
6. Scriptwriters write scripts for explainer videos.
7. UX writers write content for the UI that the customers interact with.

Creative

Creative teams have two homes in SaaS companies—the marketing department and the product department—because much of SaaS is web-based. The creative direction spills over from the brand to the product and into the realm of UI/UX design.

Creative teams that are part of marketing usually follow the structure of an agency and work as an internal agency to the various teams within the company that rely on them. They have creative directors who run all or part of the creative team and art directors who oversee the work of graphic designers (still and motion graphics are specialities). There are copywriters in the creative team as well who focus on writing very short-form copy that sits well in design. Skill sets here could encompass print, digital, static and motion graphic design that can be applied to a variety of formats like digital campaigns, events, print collateral and branded goods among others.

Creative teams in the product department as part of a UI/UX studio have skills that are rooted in web design. Here, the skills include UX research, interaction design, empathy, wireframing and UI prototyping, among others. As UX design involves interactions with the product, marketing and engineering teams, it is more collaborative than graphic design. While hiring for creative talent in marketing and UX teams, these different skill sets must be sought. Expecting someone with a print design background to be good at UI/UX design would be like judging a fish on how well it can climb a tree!

Website

The website is one of the most critical assets in a SaaS company's arsenal. The website is the product and the company. It is everything. It's where you send users or work towards users finding you. It is where you capture trial users and convert them to paid users. In SaaS companies, websites should not be treated as a corporate marketing asset but as an asset jointly owned by the marketing and product teams.

Unlike other companies, the website is a part of the business and product experience. One needs to distinguish between the pre-login and post-login website experience. Most of the post-login experience falls into the realm of the product team, but as we have seen in earlier chapters, the marketing team plays a role in crafting the right UX that gets them to use and pay for usage.

The pre-login experience is where most of the work needs to be done to improve the discoverability of the website from an SEO point of view, publish content that the buyer persona finds useful and create the right UX design that comes out in a user-friendly, warm and attractive manner to the website visitor. The visitor then proceeds to enter TOFU by signing up or subscribing to a newsletter.

The website team needs to have a combination of web design, UX design, SEO and content experience to successfully craft a website that is a solid demand generation engine.

Growth

In the SaaS world (and in other worlds), demand generation is now called growth. The term is fancier but subsumes S&M efforts to achieve growth for the company by acquiring new customers and driving expansion business. Renewals are largely a responsibility of the customer success team with minimal involvement of the sales team.

SaaS marketers are largely judged on the growth that they drive for the business. While corporate marketing has its place in creating awareness for the brand and in positioning the brand, growth is where the rubber meets the road and is the most quantifiable and measurable outcome of marketing investment.

Growth teams typically include field marketing, digital marketing, marketing operations, lead nurturing and SDR/inside sales teams, depending on the target segments that your SaaS company aims for.

Field Marketing

Field marketing is a key team to build with a focus on both large-format and small-format events where target personas from target accounts can be engaged with. Field marketers are a varied bunch, so it is important to differentiate between the tradeshow-focused team and the microformat-focused team. Additionally, if you are regionally diversified, then having a home country and regional field team is important.

Digital Marketing

Digital marketing now takes up 70 per cent of most B2B SaaS marketing spends, but it is important not to spread oneself too thin with the variety of digital channels available now. Having an experienced in-house digital marketing team is key to achieving the right balance of channel, campaign and spend. Avoid going for agencies to spend your budget! They don't have the domain knowledge or knowledge of buyer personas that you do and are happy to take a percentage of your spend as their fee. Use agencies sparingly, but build an in-house team that has specialists in the channels that give you the best return (in terms of CLTV/CAC—more on this in the chapter on metrics).

Today, digital marketers specialise in channels. You will find Google Ads specialists, Facebook and Instagram specialists, remarketing specialists, affiliate marketing experts and many more. Looking for someone with skills that go beyond just campaign and spend optimisation and a more holistic view of lead management down the funnel is important. These skills are not as common as campaign management or campaign running skills, which are a dime a dozen.

Marketing Operations

Hire this team first before you hire anyone else! The marketing operations team sets up the entire lead management system through marketing automation and integrates it with the CRM system. Platforms such as Salesforce and HubSpot, to name a few, provide marketing automation and CRM, but marketers also prefer to get best-in-class tools for automation, ABM and marketing attribution and integrate them using open architectures, which are prevalent today.

The marketing operations teams also need to have analytics and reporting specialists who can help keep track of marketing impact and productivity through relevant dashboards. Depending on your data architecture, a combination of business analysts, BI specialists, Microsoft Excel experts and specialists in Google Analytics, Google Search Console and conversion rate optimisation (CRO) is necessary to help you.

Lead Nurturing

A bona fide specialisation that needs to be a part of every SaaS growth team, lead nurturing primarily uses email and in-product messaging but can use other formats like remarketing as well. Lead nurturing experts are good at moving TOFU leads to BOFU using a combination of these channels. Lead to MQL conversion is typically the parameter on which this team is judged.

SDRs/Inside Sales

This team sits as an interface between the marketing and the sales teams. The SDRs convert MQLs into SQLs and also do outbound prospecting. SaaS companies are divided on which organisation the SDR should sit in—marketing or sales. With growth becoming the unifying function for S&M, that question is answered! SDR is a highly programmatic function that needs to be run by the book, by the clock and by the numbers. Having the SDR team as a part of marketing is key to taking end-to-end ownership of the delivery of SQLs to the sales pipeline. Otherwise, there's always scope for an excuse to say 'I gave them an MQL but *they* didn't convert'.

Product and Partner Marketing

Product marketing is not a new role and has been around as long as products have. SaaS marketers need to look at products differently as compared to the non-SaaS world. In the world of open architectures, SaaS products do not exist in isolation. They need to be interoperable with a host of other SaaS and non-SaaS systems. Secondly, the decision maker is now the user. So, product marketers need to be attuned to understanding, finding and activating users on their SaaS products.

Product organisations are also different in their orientation. In some companies, PMs perform both PM and PMM roles. In others, they are separate. In the SaaS world, they are usually separate and share a joint responsibility towards creating a go-to-market plan for a product and executing it.

Five Roles PMMs Play in a SaaS Company

Positioning, Pricing and Messaging

In a SaaS organisation, PMMs are responsible for defining how the product is positioned vis-a-vis competitors to the buyer personas. They also contribute valuable insight through surveys, interviews, competitor research and secondary research on pricing and feature decisions. The responsibility of manifesting the essence of a product on the company's external facing assets such as presentations, website, videos and social media also falls on them, in collaboration with other teams like content, creative and web.

Product Launch

While product launches are a fairly old concept and used to be accompanied by much fanfare, even in the enterprise software and hardware categories, SaaS product launches rely more on users writing about what is new, PMMs creating blogs and videos about what is new and early adopter customers providing their testimonials. The company's owned, earned and paid media channels must be leveraged to promote all this content.

Evangelism

Partnering with DevRel, the sales team and other parts of the marketing team, PMMs help to popularise the product among the buyer and user persona (most times, they are the same). They do this by hosting webinars, attending events, giving demonstrations of the product, partnering with DevRel to make the product and supporting documentation more user-friendly, contributing to the knowledge base and participating in the community.

Insight

The PMMs need to provide an outside-in perspective to the product teams. Sometimes product teams get so involved in building a product that they may not focus on whether it is the right product or the right configuration that is being built. The PMMs can conduct surveys, focus group interviews and one-on-one meetings with potential users, use secondary research, analyse competitors and provide inputs that can help guide the product and engineering effort.

Activation

Once the product is in the beta stage of the launch or even generally available, PMMs need to focus on getting more users to sign up to use the product. They can aid demand generation efforts and also work with DevRel teams to get more users via channels like hackathons, meetups and other engagement vehicles.

Partner marketing is an equally important aspect of product marketing. Traditionally, partner marketing focused on areas like reseller enablement or system integrator enablement or cloud vendor enablement (AWS, Google Cloud and Azure). However, in the SaaS world, where APIs and open architectures enable products to be integrated with a variety of systems, partners can be API marketplaces, ISVs who use APIs to build their solutions, enterprise resource planning (ERP), automation, CRM, supply chain management (SCM) and human capital management (HCM) systems that can plug into your product as part of deeper workflows and many others.

While PMMs can play the role of partner marketers, preferably, marketers should be focused on the 'ecosystem playbook' that needs to be used to ensure that your product is an integral part of the right product and market ecosystem and does not lose out to the competition. Partner marketers work on a go-to-market plan for the ecosystem where they ensure that they have built a working relationship with all the ecosystem partners that are relevant to your product and work with them on listing, joint solution development, joint marketing and demand generation campaigns.

DevRel

DevRel teams, like the SDR team, have different homes! In most companies, the DevRel team is a part of the product and engineering organisations because developers need to interact with developers and those that are knowledgeable about the product. However, DevRel is more than just getting your company's developers to meet the customer's developers!

The DevRel function is a demand generation function that makes developers aware of your product in terms of what can be done by using its APIs or integrating with it. It is a content marketing function that provides essential resources that help developers use your product for their success. It is a community-building function that connects various users of your product so that they can help each other and also generate knowledge and content on their own that can help new users. We discussed the merits of this in earlier chapters.

Hiring for a DevRel team requires you to find people who have a combination of technical skills to understand the product, marketing skills to promote it and people skills to interact with a variety of internal and external teams. They can neither be too technical nor lean more towards product promotion. Balance is the key. Within DevRel, you can hire specialists who focus on community, those that focus on content and those that focus on evangelism. If you start small, you can hire people who can do a bit of all these, but as you grow, it is better to hire specialists who can focus and deliver and scale up.

Areas That DevRel Usually Focuses On

Community

Community is the most visible manifestation of a healthy DevRel programme. The focus here is to create a space—physical and/or virtual—where users of the product can congregate and exchange ideas and feedback to help each other and generate new knowledge. The CMs focus on adding more members to the community, monitor exchanges and discussions, moderate where required and even seed conversations around new products and features.

Content

Content is the most workmanlike aspect of DevRel, something that most companies fail to focus on. High-quality user documentation and content can help users understand the product on their own and start using it without delays. Creating content that works and matters to users requires a good deal of user research, which DevRel managers need to do to produce what is relevant and usable.

Code

Developers like to be helped with code snippets and libraries to get them going on their usage journey. Identifying what is helpful, what can be shared and what they should be allowed to figure out on their own is important. Additionally, developers can be encouraged to come forward and share applications that they worked on and possibly share implementation details so that others can benefit from its addition to the knowledge base.

Start-up evangelism is another aspect of DevRel that can be explored if your business model allows for it. Most SaaS companies follow a pyramid sales model, where the focus of the sales team is on the top and the middle of the pyramid. The bottom is usually served by a self-service model (we discussed PLG earlier). The bottom of the pyramid for SaaS companies is usually composed of digital native start-ups that are pre-series A (bootstrapped, seed-funded) and could be part of incubators, cohorts of venture capital funds, government-run incubators or co-working spaces.

DevRel teams can partner with these organisations to offer start-up credits for the product for these organisations to use and explore on their own. Giving credits is a cost-effective way to acquire customers at the bottom of the pyramid who may, over time, work their way into the mid-market and enterprise sections of the pyramid. DevRel can play a key role in their acquisition.

7

Running SaaS Marketing Motions

In the previous section, we looked at how to build SaaS marketing teams, what skills to look for and how to strike a balance between generalists and specialists depending on the size and scale of your SaaS organisation. Let's look at how to 'run the business' and sometimes 'transform the business' with these teams on a daily basis.

In general, SaaS companies are in a hyper-growth or exponential growth mode. There has to be an appetite both for order and chaos, at the same time! Having programmes in place that are flexible to change but firm in their focus is key to managing SaaS marketing.

Media Relations

Whether you have one corporate communications employee, one agency, multiple employees or multiple agencies, all of them must operate within the same messaging house that you have constructed for the company. Agencies are happy to collect their retainer and deliver passable results because the agency model requires them to overcommit and stretch across multiple clients. Getting the best out of a corporate communications agency is in your hands as a SaaS marketer, not theirs.

Guidelines to Run an Effective Corporate Communications Programme

Make Your Message Newsworthy

Keeping the messaging house as your benchmark in all marketing and, especially, in corporate communication is important. This is especially true as your programme scales to cover different countries, agencies and media partners. You will need to create a newsworthy version of your message to make it more interesting to journalists because they need to write about topics that are interesting and insightful to readers. Making your message newsworthy takes skill, more than any other skill that a media relations professional can have. As discussed in the previous chapter, linking your product's capability to a megatrend like e-commerce growth in India or rise in loan defaults or an increase in employee attrition in technology companies, based on what is relevant to your product, is crucial.

Identify the Right Media Universe, Not Your Agency's Favourites

Sometimes, media relations employees and PR agencies have their journalistic favourites, individuals with whom they have a good relationship and from whom they are confident of getting coverage. Review this critically and look at journalists who have covered your segment or topic areas. Push for connections with them and coverage from them.

Identify Your Spokespersons without Overexposing the CEO

Your founder or CEO need not always be a spokesperson. Keeping them more exclusive, as your company grows, may be prudent. Have a set of three to five spokespersons who can cover broad strategy, market updates and product updates so that the CEO is not over-stretched and over-exposed.

Measure Media Relations like Demand Generation but Don't Treat a Journalist like a Customer

Find metrics to measure corporate communications. If you meet five journalists a month, create a metric around the pitch-to-publish ratio so that you can measure conversion efficiency. Media impact value is emerging as a metric that determines the value to your SaaS business from all your media placements—owned, earned and paid. Look at the correlation of coverage with direct traffic to your website and to specific product pages that are related to the topic of coverage. Journalist pitches are different from customer pitches. These pitches are about exciting them, getting them to learn first and then getting them to write. So, a journalist who wants to cover your segment may interview three or four other companies like yours before writing an industry story, which is acceptable. That's a stepping stone to an exclusive!

Benchmark Constantly

As you measure media relations performance, you need to benchmark against your competitors in your regions of operations. Tools like Meltwater and Brandwatch give you a quantified view of media mentions that your brand gets, but you can do this on your own in a more accurate and cost-efficient manner by tracking your competitor's media coverage over a month, quarter or year.

Media relations is all about focused effort, and the results will come. It is not a black art but a subtle science of how to make your stories newsworthy and interesting to journalists and readers.

AR

Once you understand how the analyst ecosystem works, AR is more of a science than media relations. Analysts speak to both customers and vendors. They are supposed to help clients choose the right vendors and vendors get the right accreditation so that they make the shortlist for clients. Also, AR requires you to pound the pavement, get your company and technology in front of the analysts and keep yourself in the consideration set whenever they write about your segment of creating a competitive landscape of vendors.

Running an AR Programme for a SaaS Company

Here are a few things to keep in mind while running an AR programme.

Understand the Business Model of Analysts

There is always an organic and paid aspect to any analyst firm. Usually, briefings are organically arranged, but if you want inputs from them, then there is a charge in the form of a subscription. For a tier-1 analyst like Gartner, the charge is quite expensive, but smaller firms do not charge as much. However, smaller firms are not read or followed by many. So, identifying the right firm, the right analysts and budgeting for spend is important. You may be covered by an analyst through free briefings, but it is a road with more friction when it comes to getting their time and focus.

Partner with the Product Team

Analysts look for not just a strategic view of your capabilities but what they can see working in action. Otherwise, they can easily assume that your products only exist on Google Slides! A strong partnership with the product team will help the AR manager get the right product narrative and demonstration in place for an analyst.

Focus, Instead of Easy Pickings

Analyst firms come in all shapes and sizes. Smaller firms might have lower barriers to entry and coverage, but larger firms require a longer gestation cycle (typically a few months to a year), which should not deter you from choosing them. Prepare internal stakeholders for a medium to long haul with larger analyst firms.

Build and Nurture Analyst Relationships

A SaaS company that takes a subscription with a tier-1 analyst firm has more than fifty interactions with their analysts in a year! These interactions include briefings (vendor presents), inquiries (vendor receives feedback), reviews (vendor shares presentations, e-books and whitepapers for review) and speaking engagements (analysts are invited to speak at vendor events). A genuine effort must be made to build meaningful and mutually insightful relationships.

Digital Marketing

Digital marketing forms a majority of SaaS marketing budgets. This team can operate efficiently in a central hub model, serving all the geographies in which the company operates. Teams and spends can be scaled up and down, and measurability is very granular with end-to-end tracking now possible from the very first click on a search advertisement, for example, right down to the CLTV.

Digital Marketing Programmes

Here are a few things to keep in mind while running digital marketing programmes.

Make Sure the Engine is Pointed in the Right Direction

Digital marketing can go horribly wrong if it operates at full scale but targets an incorrect buyer persona or segment. This scenario can happen if the channels you choose do not support the specific targeting criteria that you need to find your buyer persona.

Digital Marketers Need to be Immersed in the Business

Field marketers are usually part of triads and quads but digital marketers tend not to be. SaaS marketers need to ensure that digital marketers have a deeper understanding of buyer persona, buying behaviour, lead cycle and sales cycle, especially when they need to run ABM campaigns.

Test and Ramp Instead of Opening Flood Gates

Digital marketers tend to scale programmes quickly because it is easy to do so. Running tests with smaller spends is imperative to test not just campaign performance but also the conversion potential of leads at an MQL, SQL and closure level.

Avoid the Lookalike Trap

When digital marketers build audiences on digital channels like LinkedIn using company names and personas, the channels tend to nudge them to add lookalikes, so that there is a sizeable audience to target. However, lookalikes can dilute the focus and get accounts into the pipeline that might not meet business criteria, but campaign performance is shown as healthy!

Avoid Vanity Metrics at all Costs

Digital marketing provides a ton of metrics, but SaaS marketers need to filter them with vanity-sanity-reality filters. Impressions, clicks, cost per impression (CPM) and cost per click (CPC) are all vanity metrics. Conversions and cost per conversion (which are tracked via form fills on your landing page and transactions on your checkout page) are sanity metrics. Conversion to MQL, SQL and closure are the reality metrics, followed by metrics around billing and CLTV.

Capture as Much Information as Possible

Digital markets mostly use forms to capture lead information. These can be forms native to a channel like LinkedIn or Facebook or Instagram, or they can be on a landing page. SaaS marketers should explore alternate means of capturing as much lead information as possible through chatbots as we explored in a previous chapter.

Field Marketing

Field marketing, as compared to digital marketing, has a closer view of the business and sales dynamics because events have been the go-to format for prospecting for over a hundred years now! Wanting to attend events is intuitive both for sales representatives and marketers, and the people interactions that marketers experience give them more perspective on buyers and their considerations.

However, field marketing as a programme also tends to get stuck in a loop of events and tradeshows that seem to be bringing in TOFU leads and awareness but do not result in as many conversions as we need.

Field Programmes

Here are a few things to keep in mind while running field programmes.

Understand the Named Account List

A named account list is common to both field and digital programmes, but understanding this is crucial. If the account list is broad (thousands), that gives you the licence to go big on formats in terms of size and variety. If the account is medium-sized (hundreds), then formats have to be carefully chosen and also customised for one's requirements. If the account list is smaller (which is possible if your solution is niche and your market strategy is focused), then avoid all large formats and go only for custom formats like round tables, webinars and workshops.

Sponsorships Are Seductive, so Focus on What You Get for It

The event business has been around for decades, and they know how to create enough space for brands to maximise revenues from them. You have event sponsors, title sponsors, presenting sponsors, track sponsors, session sponsors, cocktail sponsors, bag sponsors and lanyard sponsors. Basically, every asset, physical or digital, is monetisable. Having your logo against any of them is seductive, but the focus should be on the outcomes with respect to key account lists and personas—connecting with them through preset meetings, one-on-one interactions and panel invitations among others.

Focus on a Few That Matter

Events attract all kinds of visitors, many of them irrelevant to your business. Focus on the personas from the accounts that matter to you. Don't fall into the familiar trap of measuring the number of contacts, cards and databases that you get from any event. Most of them will not convert to an SQL because they do not satisfy one or more of the BANT criteria that your SDR team needs to create an SQL out of the contact.

Create an Experience

If you invest in a booth, small or big, focus on showing what your product can do and, if possible, put it in the visitors' hands, not yours. Let them use it and play with it. Show them the real product, simulations or anything that will get to an aha moment.

Martech and Operations

Modern marketing operations run on the martech stack. Gartner estimated a few years ago that CMO spends on technology infrastructure rivals and sometimes even exceeds that of the CIO. Hiring a good marketing operations team is key to getting the martech stack built and working towards making the marketing effort efficient and delivering ROI.

Running a Marketing Operations Team

Here are a few things to keep in mind while running a marketing operations team.

Get a Fix on the Backbone

Marketing automation and CRM software are two key elements of marketing operations. A lot of decisions on operations and the stack stem from this. SaaS marketers can go with LeadSquared or HubSpot for a certain scale of operations or Marketo if they want enterprise scale for marketing automation. The CRM software is usually Salesforce but could be HubSpot as it also provides a CRM as does LeadSquared. Oracle has a complete suite as does SAP. So these systems are the first on the list to select.

Pick the People Based on the Stack

Marketing automation tools and CRM systems require specific expertise. Some people get certified and specialise in configuring and optimising on these platforms. Once you build the backbone, planning for scale is important. For example, any transition out of Marketo to Oracle can necessarily mean changing key personnel because skill sets are different.

Have an Integration Strategy in Place

With open architectures, most platforms are interoperable, but the difficulty levels vary. Platforms that combine marketing automation and CRM like to keep end-to-end control of the marketing and sales funnel and offer limited integration capabilities, while others offer more flexibility with connectors for integration. Exploring integration marketplaces like Zapier is also important, where direct one-to-many integration is not necessary but can be done via Zapier, which has already built connectors with many systems.

Focus on Data Clean-Ups Before Reporting

One of the biggest issues that marketing operations need to deal with is data inconsistency. This inconsistency happens when prospects enter junk into forms or when field marketing hands in forms filled by attendees from an event where key fields like email or mobile number are missing. One of the biggest services that the marketing operations team needs to provide the company is to clean the data *early* so that incomplete leads don't find their way deep into the funnel.

Bring Operations Closer to the Front Line

The marketing operations team should ideally also manage the MOFU campaigns. Marketing automation drives emails, which are the primary nurture vehicles. This way, they also have a play in the whole demand generation machinery and are not passive observers who do not have a stake in it. They also provide an ideal feedback mechanism for digital and field marketers on the quality of leads their campaigns bring in.

Product and Partner Marketing

The PMM and partner marketing teams need to be deeply integrated with the product and engineering organisations. Many SaaS companies have product councils that connect regularly to take stock of larger movements in the roadmap, and product and partner marketing needs to be an essential part of those. If your SaaS company has a chief product officer or VP of product, involving them in decisions regarding the composition and selection of this team is crucial to fostering a spirit of partnership.

Running a PMM and Partner Marketing Organisation

Avoid Over-Reliance on the Product Team

Containing the level of reliance may seem counter-intuitive, but PMMs fall into the trap of looking over their shoulders and seeking PM approvals. Product managers are like product CEOs, but they are not product CMOs. Decisions on positioning, messaging, pricing, launching and content creation around a product should remain with the PMM while working closely with the PM.

Be a Co-Owner of the Product, not a Support Team

PMMs need to own the go-to-market strategy for a product. They should critically evaluate the buyer persona it is meant for. They need to determine how and where to find target personas, how to position the product to them, where to make the product visible and how to help users start using. They should also help in acquiring user perspective on improving current features and getting new feature ideas.

PMMs Need to be Good Writers and Communicators

Over-reliance on content writers to create product content can be counterproductive. While the SaaS marketing team needs to be conversant with the product, a content writer will never know more about a product than a PMM. However, a PMM can be equally good, if not better, writer than a content writer. This skill is often overlooked while hiring PMMs but manifests itself quite quickly in the spoken and written work that is turned out.

Insert PMMs into Every Speaking and Demonstration Possible

Field events provide the best opportunity for this, as do webinars. The more PMMs interact with potential customers, the better their inputs to the product and positioning of the product will be. PMMs also need to be part of customer success calls as observers so that they can experience the onboarding process and activation process. They can also interact with the product group that manages the self-service motion so that they can see how self-service users react to features and the product experience.

Integrate with Technology, Integration and Resell Partners

Partner marketers need to work closely with organisations outside the company and connect with peers from technology partner companies, integration companies that the SaaS product needs to integrate with and resellers like ISVs who use the product to build custom solutions for their clients. These peers need to be on their speed dial!

DevRel

DevRel, as we saw in the previous chapter, interfaces with product and engineering teams on the inside and users and developers on the outside. They are to users what PMMs are to buyers in that they make it easy for users to understand the product and its benefits, how to try it out, how to use it for one's benefit and how to get help from others (the community) that uses it. DevRel should be managed by the marketing organisation and not the technology organisation.

Running a DevRel Team

Do the Dirty Work First

Developers require basics to be in place if you want them to use your product. That means documentation, code snippets, videos, a support line and a good UX. Instead of community building as a primary objective, get your team to have this in place first to an acceptable level.

Collect Feedback to Inform Decisions

In case your self-service system and documentation are not up to scratch, the DevRel team needs to conduct hackathons and capture feedback from users to drive the direction of UX and documentation. They become the 'voice of the developer' within the company.

Start Small Before You Scale

If your community is in its nascent stage, start collecting user details from customer support databases and sales contacts or product login databases to start the first level of interactions to test the waters. For each person who comes in, ask them to bring a friend who is a developer so you can grow your network.

Create Internal Heroes Before External Ones

DevRel needs a close partnership with the product and engineering organisations, but the problem is they may not be inspired or incentivised to spend their time answering community questions or helping you write API documentation or creating content for a developer webinar. Make your helpers heroes before you make developers heroes.

8

Working with SaaS Founders

Most SaaS companies are less than ten years old. At that age and stage, the company is still run and driven by the (co)founders and the founding team. While a lot has been said about entrepreneurs and the fire and passion and guts and gumption with which they build their companies, against all odds, very little has been written about how to work with them and for them!

Why is that important? SaaS marketers may not always be co-founders or members of the founding or early-stage team. They are mostly professional managers working for a SaaS company co-founded by someone else. Depending on seniority, they may report to the co-founder or a member of the founding team or someone who reports to them.

SaaS companies provide wonderful growth opportunities for a marketer, but one's mindset needs to change to work in them. Here are a few things to remember.

Working for a SaaS Start-Up

Change is on an Overdrive

Strategy, people, operations and culture also can change in a matter of months. Keep calm and ride the storm. Clarity usually emerges through chaos. Until SaaS companies achieve an annual recurring revenue (ARR) of US$1 million, they constantly experiment and hustle to find the product market fit and the right customer base. If you are a marketer in this set-up, be ready to try and fail forward if you do!

The Sword of Damocles

Not all SaaS companies are resource-rich. So they tend to reduce their workforce if a few quarters don't go their way. Learning to function under this sword is key. Working under pressure is the best teacher. One of the advantages of SaaS is that it appreciates the life cycle view of a customer. Hence, marketers need not always rely on spending to add to TOFU but can focus on strengthening content motions, self-service motions, freemium motions and trial motions to get relevant leads into the system, even during difficult times.

Structure Gives Way

Structure usually gives way to make things happen. Larger companies are enslaved by structure because they can't function without it. Smaller SaaS companies have loose exoskeletal structures that are there to avoid descending into chaos but are flexible enough to come together for the successful completion of a task or project. If you have worked for a larger company and are moving into a smaller SaaS company, keep structure in your mind but also be flexible!

Let's look at how SaaS marketers can work with founders and founding teams and deal with organisational dynamics.

The SaaS Founder as a Manager

Reporting to or working for a SaaS founder can be an adventure—exhilarating, challenging and scary but ultimately fulfilling if you know what to expect and how to handle it. Founders appreciate the qualities that they have in themselves. Passion, grit, flexibility, courage and stamina are some that come to mind. If you closely analyse the founding team of a SaaS company, you will find the same qualities in them, plus a few more, which we will explore in the next few sections!

Some SaaS companies have multiple founders. They usually have complementary skills so that the combined founding team is well-rounded. If one is more technology-savvy, the other is more market-savvy and the third might be oriented towards operations. Understanding how they see the SaaS business is important to win their confidence.

How SaaS Managers Can Work with the Co-Founders of a Company

Co-Founders Love Their Companies

Co-founders are passionate, hardworking and driven to make their companies succeed—all good things a SaaS marketer can learn from and imbibe. The hours are 24/7, not 9 to 5. You may or may not love the company the way they do, but you need to respect their love for it. What every co-founder wants you to do is to believe in the company's mission, purpose and reason to exist. As a marketer, you need to use that as the roof of your messaging house, a concept we discussed in earlier chapters.

Love also complicates matters. As a marketer, you will bring a lot of ideas to the table, and at times, you may find that many of those ideas are either shot down or pushed out. Founders are so used to owning and controlling all aspects of the business that they find it hard to let go and let others drive some aspects!

Love versus Objectivity

This conflict plays out specifically when a brand wants to, needs to or has been told to pivot. That's the true test of a founder's willingness to change. If you are a driver of that change, then you need to be aware of this conflict and the inertia that comes with it and help the founder gain confidence. This situation can also play out in routine decisions like choosing a colour scheme for the brand or deciding what words a press release should have or even what the company t-shirt design should be.

This conflict can test your patience as a marketer, especially if you have known your suggestions to work in other companies. It can lead to conflict and frustration. You must guard against this discord because you can become unpopular very soon. The one dissonant voice tends to stand out! So, how do you combat that?

Control versus Confidence

Founders know a fair bit about all aspects of running a company—sales, marketing, finance and technology. At some point, they would have worked on all these functions. When they hire professional managers like you, the SaaS marketer, they need to have confidence in you to let you handle what you are qualified to handle! The way to win their confidence is to focus on small wins. Take a small task and show that you can do it well. Then take another and another, until you get to a point where, suddenly, no one stops you or asks you too much because you handle them well. This approach works well for smaller tasks and projects.

For larger projects like a brand refresh, a repositioning or a website redesign, you must show a POC, the research and the work and get the founding team to buy in. Then, try the idea out on a staging platform, again show it, show the work and get feedback. Make them comfortable and part of the process. Once they get the confidence that you can handle 'their baby', you will have more freedom as you build more confidence.

Challenging versus Complying

While these approaches seem to be at the opposite ends of the spectrum, SaaS marketers must choose their battles wisely in terms of when to challenge a founder's long-cherished notion and when to accept it (despite disagreeing with it). Often, founders *don't know* the finer points of marketing or digital campaigns or lead nurturing.

So when you explain, they may gloss over it or not realise the importance of implementing it. Pick areas that you feel are critical (like choosing a marketing automation platform) to hold your ground and leave other areas (like t-shirt colour) as some things that you can live with even when things don't go your way.

Co-founders also trust their founding team implicitly. Let's look at how to work with founding teams.

Founding Teams

Not much has been said or written about working with the founding team. The founding team does not have the title of founder or co-founder but has been instrumental in starting and building the company. They have exhibited the same qualities that founders value. Notably, they may not be the most skilled in what they do but they have bucketfuls of the right attitude!

Founding teams have the full confidence and backing of their founders, which will always be more than the backing you enjoy. If this is your first small company, then you may find it hard to digest, especially at a senior level. However, you need to understand and navigate the situation.

Working with a Founding Team

DON'T IGNORE THEM

Founding teams are here to stay, and they have built the business, in all fairness. While you may not spend a lot of time with the co-founders, you will encounter the founding team everywhere. Newcomers make the mistake of saying that now that they have been hired, they will run the show. As SaaS companies grow, marketers are hired to work alongside founding team members who played the role before and sometimes to manage them or report to them, which can create quite a bit of unrest and friction! SaaS marketers need to be aware of the founding team.

Understand the Dynamics of Influence

The centre of gravity of every group—old versus new, senior versus junior, function versus function, executive versus executive—is different. This dynamic gives you a picture of who to build relationships with and convince if you want key decisions and results to be implemented. Sometimes, to convince the founder of a marketing decision, you will need to convince the people that the founder trusts. Feedback flows in SaaS companies in all directions, and there is always a buzz around who is new. Make sure that you identify the influencers of opinion and work with them.

Understand What Has Been Done and Appreciate It

There's always a chance that you enter a SaaS company as a marketer and find many things non-existent or broken. You must never publicly insult or critique what's been done before or those that were behind it. Understanding when to and when not to do this is a learning curve, and to win over the founding team, you need to acknowledge the work they did to get the company to where it is. Of course, acknowledging doesn't mean resorting to sycophancy, and a balance must be maintained.

Evolve Their Roles and Leverage Their Strengths

Founding teams can be powerful allies who can help you navigate the complexities of the SaaS organisation. Finding data residing in silos, information flows broken, people sitting on insight and not sharing it openly and so on is not uncommon, but with the right founding team partnership, you will find that the sea parts in front of you! Information is key, and the founding team can be a conduit to finding it for you.

Communicate the 'Why' as Much as the 'What'

Don't get so busy implementing initiatives that you forget the importance of explaining and communicating why a particular marketing initiative is important. 'Because I said so' is not a good enough answer, especially when you are new. Focus more on the 'why' and evangelise your idea, instead of bursting in with the 'what'.

You and Your Work Need to Do the Talking

In the long run, only those who perform will be left standing and consistently growing. You need to ensure that people know what you do. Be a communicator to cut through the cobweb of organisational dynamics but also take care to ensure you don't come across as a prima donna. SaaS marketers need to walk a thin line!

However, not everything is difficult. Once you break through the barriers mentioned earlier and form a good, trust-based working relationship with the founders and the founding team, you can leverage their strengths and your experience to execute some great marketing programmes for your SaaS company.

New versus Old

We touched upon the founders and the founding team and how they seem to be a harmonious unit whose wavelength and outlook towards business and life, in general, are the same. A 'tribe culture' gets built with that core group. As SaaS companies grow, the tribe might disperse into different teams and different leaders, but they are very much in touch with one another, looking at and observing the way the company is growing, the new people who are joining in and the way 'their baby' is growing.

Most SaaS marketers join the company as professional managers who are not founders or founding team members and face what is known as the 'new versus old' battle. A founding team needs to change with the times but rarely does. Founders feel that if this team can take us from zero to one, they can take us from one to ten and ten to hundred as well. The truth is, though, 'horses for courses'. Scale is not everyone's cup of tea, and slugging it out with no resources isn't everyone's cup of tea either. People have skills and experience that suit certain things. As the saying goes, you can't judge a fish by its ability to climb a tree.

SaaS companies with practical and forward-looking board members and founders will not fall into this trap. They will proactively bring in new talent at all levels and leverage the strength of the founding team by finding appropriate roles for them. They do bring in new talent, but they leave it halfway done. That is, they correctly see the need to bring in new talent 'from outside', but they don't consider what it does to the people who 'are inside'. The emphasis on these words is because newcomers are not automatically welcomed into the tribe. They need to earn their spot. There's no one to help them do that unless a conscious effort is made to help them integrate.

One of the reasons this initiative is left incomplete is that the founders don't want to deal with the conflicts that arise from bringing in new professionals from outside either to work alongside or manage members of the founding team. Sometimes, the tribe is not taken into confidence when a professional is hired from the outside. Other times they are, but the decision is met with resistance. Then they decide to give in because the board may have insisted and the founder tells them to go with the decision.

The conflict between old and new can lead to a passive-aggressive approach or an openly aggressive approach taken towards newcomers in the SaaS organisation. The best companies create a culture within the company where no one is bigger than the company, not even the founders. That culture opens up minds to the fact that what they are building is bigger than any of them and that change—in the form of new people, new investors, new offices, new locations and new organisational structure—contributes ultimately to achieving the mission of the company.

How SaaS Marketers Can Tackle the Old versus New Problem

Acknowledge the Incumbents

Those that have done the work before you joined must be acknowledged. They may have been marketers of some grade or non-marketers who have stepped in to play the role. A new entrant, especially a leader, makes them feel insecure and even unwanted. That kind of feeling can fester if not addressed. So, start with an acknowledgment.

Understand Their Strengths

While most of the incumbents might have worked on multiple marketing projects, they may be good at one over the other. Understand those strengths, leverage them and bring in specialists for what's lacking. Having a team of generalists is not scalable in a SaaS marketing organisation, considering the expertise required in the organisation.

Urge the Founder to Help with the Transition

Helping with the transition is essential but most founders do not. In all fairness, they may think that it is not a great use of their time. However, at least for senior hires, getting the founder to sit in on the first two transition meetings will be useful to help incumbents cope with the change.

Make Them Feel a Part of Future Growth

Once strengths are identified, assigning roles that are commensurate with the capabilities of the incumbents and that drive future marketing growth will make them feel an equal part of the future as compared to the past.

Inheriting versus Building

Building a new SaaS marketing team from scratch is the ideal case for a SaaS marketer to lay the foundations for the entire framework that we have discussed in this book. If you get such an opportunity, you should grab it with both hands. However, these scenarios are rare and you end up inheriting some form of a marketing organisation that you need to shape, polish and (re)build.

Things to Remember While Inheriting a SaaS Marketing Team

Look at What's Working

SaaS marketers tend to go in and start ripping and replacing so that the organisation looks exactly like what's in our minds. However, every company is different, and understanding what's working well in the existing marketing team and not disturbing it immediately but in a considered manner, over time, is important.

Centralise Dispersed Resources

If the company you join has dispersed marketing resources, moving them into your organisation, while they continue to serve the teams that they do, is advisable. This is the first step to bringing order, process and consistency into existing marketing efforts. This movement can lead to consternation from those that they currently report to, but it is a bitter pill that needs to be swallowed early.

Win with Insight, Not Authority

If you want your inherited team to respect you, do so with insight. In every review and every meeting, provide insights that can help them do their jobs better. Better still, ask them where they need help, instead of telling them that they need help!

Avoid 'Your' People

SaaS marketers tend to bring in former colleagues who they are comfortable working with into a team that they have inherited, which can be a recipe for disaster. As human beings, we are inclined to trust people we know and have been in the trenches with; team members we have hired and groomed. Bringing them in makes sense when you are building a team from scratch but not when you are inheriting one. It disturbs the fault lines like old versus new and insider versus outsider, which you should avoid.

Occupational Hazards of Being a SaaS Marketer

Everyone Thinks They Know Your Job Better than You

Yes, from the janitor and above, everyone, and I mean everyone, has a 'well-informed' opinion on Marketing 101 and specifically on what you do. Everyone relates to marketing and has an opinion. You won't find that with the finance or supply chain or IT functions because not everyone relates to them.

Despite all the Data, Justifying Your Impact Is Challenging

Even with sophisticated marketing data and attribution in place, marketing contribution is often consumed with a truckload of salt. Over and above this, good relationships need to be built with your stakeholders such as the CEO and the heads of sales, product, customer success, finance (yes!) and HR functions. Attribution models need to be signed off by the sales and the finance departments so that you can justify ROI on your spend.

Despite all this, SaaS marketing provides a tremendous opportunity to build a brand and create a marketing framework that takes a life cycle view of a customer.

9

Marketing in the SaaS Ecosystem

SaaS companies are highly specialised and need to integrate with other SaaS companies and platforms to fit into the customer's technology ecosystem. SaaS companies need to be aware of the ecosystem that they need to be a part of to provide a holistic solution to their customers. This ecosystem consists of other SaaS and non-SaaS vendors, plugin providers, ERP systems, ISVs and even alpha software developers. For this to work, all these companies open up their programming interfaces.

Today, SaaS buyers have, on average, fifteen to twenty SaaS applications in their technology ecosystem, and they expect your product to work seamlessly with the other products they use. As a SaaS marketer, you need to help your company plug into the most comprehensive business-tech environment so that the customer sees your product as a seamless part of a holistic solution. If such an environment does not exist, then you can help create one with a network of technology partners.

Being part of a SaaS ecosystem can provide you access to more customers, buyers and influencers of today. This network can help you irrespective of your size but especially if you are a smaller SaaS company that does not yet have the field team to find customers at scale. It also helps you focus on the specific problem that you want to solve without having to replicate what other niche companies have solved for the customer.

SaaS companies realise that a single product cannot provide all the feature combinations that a customer may desire in the area of, for example, marketing. So they focus on a specific area, such as campaign optimisation, and integrate with all the other tools for campaign management, personalisation and others. SaaS companies need to be specialised and, in some cases, hyper-specialised.

Specialisation is happening in the customer ecosystem. To drive operational efficiencies and cost savings, applications that once operated in silos in functions like marketing, sales, customer success, customer support and finance are being seamlessly integrated and fused for 360-degree visibility and, of course, better collaboration. One of the key drivers for this collaboration to work, especially with ten to twenty external SaaS partners, is integration.

Customers expect integrations to be a table stakes offering and do not want to pay for integration support. They want to spare their budgets and reduce dependency on in-house developers so that integrations can be done in a matter of weeks or months instead of years. SaaS companies are working on making their core product and third-party applications work seamlessly through APIs. They are also integrating with API aggregators who provide a type of middleware-like platform that can enable disparate products to talk to one another, Zapier being a good example.

To facilitate integrations, e-commerce has created a SaaS app ecosystem that is integrated with platforms like Shopify, Magento, WooCommerce and others. Merchants can avail a host of marketing, promotion, payment, delivery and support capabilities provided by SaaS companies that work seamlessly through APIs.

SaaS marketers can help create the right ecosystem for their company by keeping the end user's journey at the centre. The customer's workflow should be simplified so that they don't need to switch through multiple screens or logins to complete a specific task like running a campaign or accessing a dashboard. Mapping the core task to be completed helps your company decide what ideal third-party partner(s) would look like.

Typically, SaaS companies use three types of integrations to plug into the ecosystem. Depending on how they want the integrations to be set up, they can provide open APIs, plug into integration platforms like Zapier or build native integrations. In the open API model, SaaS marketers must focus on building good documentation that covers use cases, demonstrations, protocols, guides, code snippets and reference frameworks.

Building a connector for integration makes it easy for your customer to integrate your product with a few clicks. Native integrations take the longest to execute, require time and resources and should only be done if the customer is strategic.

While choosing ecosystem partners, a smooth flow of data across multiple apps should be ensured. Not all SaaS products work well with each other. Configuring a product to trigger an action in another one can be challenging and needs close collaboration between ecosystem partners. Data integration and customer session integrity also need to be maintained across different products.

While building this ecosystem of partners, SaaS companies need to provide APIs and a self-service developer journey so that they can get added to newer ecosystems organically. This requires, as we have seen, sandboxes, test drive data, documentation, code snippets, videos and a reward and recognition mechanism for developers to feel inspired to come in and start building with your APIs.

With the emergence of the three main cloud providers, marketplaces have merged as a significant discovery platform for SaaS products and APIs. Marketplaces allow customers to discover the depth of the SaaS ecosystem and provide an opportunity for large and small SaaS companies to showcase their capability for discovery. Apart from third-party marketplaces, SaaS marketers should also focus on building their own marketplace for ISV apps and partner apps to be showcased and discovered. Having your own marketplace creates both an economic impact for ecosystem partners as well as a long-term competitive advantage.

Now, SaaS marketing becomes more than just your company or your product. The team that you work with is not just on your company's payroll but spread across the ecosystem that helps you market, sell, integrate and extend your products. Apart from partners that use your APIs to build, channel partners provide last-mile customer attention needed for complex implementations.

There are challenges to ecosystem marketing. Direct customer touch is not always guaranteed, which is, in many ways, the reason you are part of an ecosystem. It is a mindset shift. You will need to train your partners so that they can handle customer conversations on your behalf. There is a temptation to try and reach all customer segments, but that can be detrimental to your partners. The right balance needs to be struck to ensure that you set your partners up for success as well.

As you scale up your SaaS company, you cannot serve all segments equally. You want to avoid spreading yourself too thin and focus more on the highest potential accounts while leveraging other organisations that already have a presence in different segments, have a sales and support team and can build solutions using your products. Sometimes, in a trade-off, investment in a large go-to-market team can come at the expense of investing in product innovation and research and development (R&D). The temptation to do everything in-house will always be there, but with that comes the risk of losing focus trying to build three different sales models, four different marketing models, ten different vertical go-to-market motions and so on.

SaaS companies need to focus on the core product experience tailored to buyer personas both in a high-touch sales motion and in a PLG motion. To expand the go-to-market motion, they can invest in ecosystem partnerships. If your SaaS model is based on consumption and volumes, the focus should be on increasing that metric without spreading limited resources too thin. For example, in certain markets, businesses operate through one-to-one conversations in local languages. Here, instead of hiring a skeletal sales team and experimenting, choose a strong regional partner who knows the beats of conducting business there and test the waters for a fraction of the cost.

One area that SaaS companies don't use partners for is customer success. They build strong in-house teams that train partners, but eventually, the partner manages the last mile. Not training them to be good at customer success could be counterproductive. Creating a hub-and-spoke model with an in-house customer success hub and a distributed customer success hub across partners is more scalable than wanting to manage all end customer interactions in-house.

Most SaaS companies have 10 per cent of their feature catalogue earning 80 per cent of their revenue. These are the most common use cases that the company and customer both know they need, and you can build a solid product roadmap to satisfy that need. Still, there will always be customers with specialised use cases as your customer base and variety grows. Suddenly, you will have many feature requests that you can't and don't want to handle. You want to focus on what's core. By creating an open API or framework that your ISV partners can plug into, you can leverage their help to serve those specialised needs.

These value-added solutions make your core product stickier. These customised implementations have a higher barrier to churn because they have time, effort and resources invested in solving a very specific need. At any stage of your SaaS journey, ISV solutions are a great way to accelerate growth. Additionally, if you offer those ISV solutions on a marketplace created by you, a virtuous cycle of innovation and revenue realisation is created.

Ultimately, ecosystems are a company of companies. SaaS marketers know how to leverage the strength of the ecosystem and play as a team across different teams. Building trust-based and information-based relationships with the ecosystem is crucial to creating an open architecture and making it work seamlessly. SaaS marketers can be at the forefront of creating a robust ecosystem strategy that strengthens your business, allows you to serve more and varied customers, creates stickiness for your product and adds more and more value to your customers so that they can grow with you by their side (the life cycle view that is core to SaaS).

10

Measuring SaaS Marketing

As we've gone through various aspects of marketing for a SaaS business, the focus on metrics and measurement is apparent. More than any other business, SaaS allows you to measure marketing effectiveness, productivity and outcome at all levels and all stages of the customer life cycle. In this section, we discuss the common metrics that SaaS businesses use to measure business performance and functional performance.

Common SaaS Marketing Metrics

Start with unique monthly visitors (UMV) because SaaS products are largely web-based and bringing in targeted traffic is the first step in filling the funnel. The number of visitors who land on your website every month through organic searches, paid advertisements or direct visits is termed UMV. This metric helps to identify where visitors come from, how they behave on your website and what types of visitors have the best engagement. Visitors are measured by UMV, not sessions, because one visitor can have multiple sessions.

Not all UMVs turn into users or conversions, but this metric helps to increase brand awareness and brand mentions. An increase in site traffic also helps to increase domain authority on Google, which produces better search results provided you are doing SEO right. This increase will impact conversions positively across enterprise customers, mid-market and the long tail.

Paid marketing can be used to drive up UMV, but the goal should be to drive it up organically, that is, when people search on Google. Know the set of keywords that are core to your business and work on a content strategy that incorporates good SEO practices to ensure that they rank in the top seven results at any point in time for any given language. Achieving this ranking performance is a tall order but worth investing in. A content strategy that combines content production with content promotion is ideal to make sure that your potential customers find you in organic search results when they search for answers.

Mapping content to buyer stages (TOFU, MOFU and BOFU) is important so that you provide a variety based on what stage of the buying and evaluation journey the customer is on. Tools like Google Analytics and Google Search Console are good to get expertise on and use to drive up UMV from both branded keywords (keywords that have your company's name in them) and non-branded keywords (keywords that do not have your company's name in them).

Metrics around the lead nurture sequence are next. Once leads come into the system, they are, based on the source and the campaign, nurtured for some time before being passed on to the inside sales team for qualification. Metrics like open rate, click-through rate, percentage of opens that clicked and so on are useful to target to evaluate the quality of the nurture programme.

Tracking MQLs is crucial as that is the first tangible outcome of the marketing team. Leads who have an interest in evaluating your SaaS solution are termed MQLs. As a marketer, you score them to indicate their level of readiness to engage with sales or to get access to the product to use it on their own. Irrespective of whether they downloaded a gated e-book, filled out a contact form, subscribed to your newsletter or visited product pages, they all go through a nurture programme and are scored for being an MQL. As an example, contact-us forms can be assigned the highest score and newsletter subscriptions the lowest score. The MQL quality is a direct determinant of the quality of the sales pipeline and CLTV further down the line.

Being clear on the buyer personas that you target with your marketing campaigns, having persona-based nurtures and looking at how they are performing are key to driving MQLs upward. In these nurtures, deliver lead hooks like interesting blogs, videos and opinions that leads will respond to and value to learn first and then try out.

Trails are useful to track as a marketer if you have a freemium version or a test drive version of your product that can be run in a self-service mode. If the number of active trials constantly grows, that's a sign of actionable TOFU momentum. Tracking the velocity of leads is also a good way of seeing how fast leads move through different phases of the marketing and sales funnel.

Once MQLs go to the inside sales teams, they have their own set of metrics in terms of inbound MQLs received, percentage contacted, percentage qualified, percentage rejected and percentage converted to measure efficiency, quality of leads and productivity. The inside sales team generates SQLs, who are prospects who have shared their interest, ability to spend, decision-making process and requirements and are ready to speak to a salesperson to work on taking the opportunity now through the deal phases. Usually, companies follow a process of four to seven steps such as qualification, proposal, negotiation, contract and closure.

In the PLG model, MQLs are directed to use the product in a self-service mode and become product qualified leads

(PQLs). MQLs become PQLs based on usage behaviours in the freemium zone, and scoring is done based on behaviours demonstrated.

Conversion rates are the next set of metrics that SaaS marketers should measure. Conversion happens from lead to MQL, MQL to SQL/PQL, SQL to different lead stages and, finally, to closures. This waterfall view also shows where the efficiencies and inefficiencies are in the system. You could be generating leads efficiently, but qualification may not match that efficiency. Movement through the sales pipeline also may not match the qualification efficiency.

Conversion rates can be measured daily, weekly, monthly and beyond. If the sales team closes only a handful of SQLs, then they may be qualified too lightly, and there might be a need to increase the MQL scoring system.

Post-conversion stickiness can be measured via customer churn rate, which is the percentage of customers who stop using or do not renew their subscriptions. SaaS forces you to be a co-traveller with your customer all along their journey. Retaining customers requires a razor-sharp focus on their experience with the product and onboarding and support. A churn rate greater than 5 per cent is a cause for worry. Marketing can help get feedback from customers who have churned, look at improving onboarding, documenting and being more proactive when it comes to customer success. It is a combined effort with the triad and quad.

Normally, this metric supports product and UX teams. If the product team is tightly integrated with the triads and the quads, churn should not be caused due to a broken UX. Other areas to look at are the customer expectations that are being built up owing to the company's messaging and build-up of unreal expectations of value.

For active customers, tracking MRR is useful to track revenue being generated from marketing efforts every month. SaaS earns revenue in smaller chunks over a period. This is a sanity metric that tells you how much you bill and, when compared to previous months, tells you a deeper story than most of the other metrics.

The overall MRR for the company is a sum-product of the individual account's billing for the month at their given rate of subscription. The average revenue per account (ARPA) is the MRR divided by the total number of accounts that contributed to the MRR. Averages can be deceptive. So you can use median also if you want a clearer picture. Another way to calculate ARPA is ACV, and it is used when your business has multiple-year plans that it offers customers. It derives the total contract value across years.

If you calculate MRR, ARR can be calculated by multiplying it by 12. Now MRR and ARR can come from new accounts or existing accounts. So, keep that in mind and drive more from existing accounts.

Now that the revenue side of things is being tracked, the next thing to track is the cost incurred to acquire a customer. The amount spent on acquiring a new customer is CAC. If this is calculated across sources of leads, then we can determine which channels provide us with the best ROI for the marketing spend. Using CAC wisely can lead to looking at the most productive channels and optimising marketing spend.

Otherwise, continuing to spend on one's favourite channel without realising what is being delivered is tempting. To calculate CAC, the company's S&M expenses are divided by the number of new customers acquired during the given period. Depending on the lag, that is, the amount of time it takes for a lead to close, the expenses of an earlier period can be taken to get a more accurate picture of CAC.

Only calculating MRR or ARR limits your view to a short time. SaaS businesses need to keep customers billing and growing over years! Here, CLTV plays an important role. is the revenue that you earn from your active existing customers is termed CLTV. When divided by CAC, it gives you the multiple on the acquisition costs that you achieve. When this is broken down by marketing channel, you can optimise spends on individual channels. The CLTV is also a measure of customer longevity. Higher CLTV shows that more renewals take place or usage takes place.

Calculating CLTV needs you to determine the average customer lifetime (ACL) by dividing 1 by your churn rate. If your monthly churn is 7 per cent, your ACL would be 14.3 (1/0.07). Calculate the ARPA by dividing your MRR by the total number of active accounts. Multiply that by 12 to get ARPA. The CLTV is calculated by multiplying ACL by ARPA. As churn goes down and retention goes up, CLTV goes up.

Both CLTV and CAC are not straightforward to calculate when you have multiple marketing channels working in tandem or even sequentially—Google advertisements, LinkedIn advertisements, email marketing campaigns, paid partnerships, marketing automation tools and so on. Usually, a CLTV/CAC ratio of three and above is acceptable. The way to keep the ratio going up is to focus on retaining and expanding customers to boost the CLTV and to make the marketing, inside sales and sales functions more efficient to drive down CAC.

Now that lead and revenue metrics are covered, SaaS marketers should also look at product metrics around the pirate metrics framework (AARRR—Acquisition, Activation, Revenue, Retention, Referral).

Activations and sign-ups on the website are important metrics to track. Sign-ups are a good place to start, but unless users fill a wallet or do something to qualify as active, they don't mean much. User activities vary depending on the nature of your product but are an indication of a user deriving value from using a product. Personalised or tech-touch onboarding can help to drive up activations. Activities can also be referred to as PQLs.

However, activations do not mean revenue. Users can use a free or forever-free model and not pay you a dime. By using tracking codes to measure in-product user movements, activations can be linked directly to your digital spend.

If you offer free plans, tracking the conversion of free users to paid users is important. Sometimes, companies provide a prefilled wallet with a small amount to get users started. Any top-ups on the wallet can be a good metric to track. This metric will also tell you if you acquire more users with a sign-up mentality versus activation mentality versus paying mentality. By tracking this conversion, you can predict paid conversions from a cohort of sign-ups, track ROI from campaigns designed to drive sign-ups and provide feedback to the product teams to improve the UX towards key moments in the user journey.

Working with CSMs to track NPS also helps to identify detractors who rate between zero and six, those that are passive and those who rate between seven and eight, and promoters who rate between nine and ten. The percentage of promoters minus the percentage of distractors is termed NPS. Though it does not give direct feedback to a SaaS marketer, NPS is a good marker to have to see the kind of customers the company acquires and retains.

While working with CSMs and RMs, the retention rate is also an important metric to measure. Retention can be customer retention and/or revenue retention. Revenue retention shows the expansion or contraction of the business. Customer retention shows how many accounts have been retained. However, reducing churn is not the only way to increase revenue retention. Your existing customers may still not grow. A lot of focus should go into expansion programmes to increase the revenue retention that can be impacted by churn, inactive customers and other factors in the business.

SaaS marketers must use this data to derive marketing sourced revenue (MSR) to build a better business case for increasing marketing spend and hiring more marketers.

11

In Conclusion

We've been on some journey through the last six chapters. At times, you may have felt that we have discussed things beyond the realm of marketing and gone into the realm of business in general, but that's what SaaS is all about. A whole company comes together for one single purpose—to acquire customers, nurture them, grow revenue and renew, expand and leverage the value delivered to gain more customers. Rinse and repeat.

A few more facets remain to be covered, maybe in other books or editions—brand building, product marketing, product design, AR and media communications. What is addressed here is the core of what a SaaS marketer should do to be a vital part of a SaaS business.

Notes

1 Sheth, A., A. Shukla, P. Kashyap and G. Ericson. 'India SaaS Report 2021'. Available at: https://www.bain.com/insights/india-saas-report-2021/ (accessed on 7 December 2021).

2 SlideShare. 29 April 2022. 'Inventing Product-led Growth'. Available at: https://www.slideshare.net/OpenViewVenturePartners/inventing-productled-growth (accessed in January 2022).

3 Foley, J. (dir.). 1992. *Glengarry Glen Ross*. Los Angeles: Zupnik Enterprises.

4 Malzberg, E. 'Saas Growth Strategy #3: Cross-Selling for Increased Revenue and Retention'. Available at: https://www. zuora.com/guides/saas-growth-strategy-3-cross-sellingincreased-revenue-retention/.

Index

About the Author

Srinivas B. Vijayaraghavan is a marketing leader with over twenty years of experience in running marketing for global technology companies. Srinivas has worked in software development, marketing and business development with global technology companies like IBM, HP, Tejas Networks, Mobileum, Brillio, Pluralsight, Qubole and Gupshup. He is currently the CMO of Loop. He has been a SaaS marketer for the past eight years.

Srinivas's marketing experience cuts across brand management, positioning, digital and field-led demand generation, customer marketing, PR and content management. He has worked across IT, telecom, SaaS and e-commerce domains.

He is the author of two business books—*Marketing for Services Outsourcing* and *Filmy Manager*.

Srinivas has an MBA from the Indian Institute of Management (IIM) Bangalore and an engineering degree in computer science from PES Institute of Technology (now PES University), Bengaluru. He is currently pursuing a PhD at IIM Kozhikode. He also has two granted patents from the United States Patent and Trademark Office. He has over 100 hours of teaching in marketing management and business communications at Alliance University, Bengaluru. He was a member of the advisory board on executive education at Dayanand Sagar University, Bengaluru. Srinivas plays the drum and bass guitar.